Mehdi's
Fast-Track
Success System Workbook

Form the habits that will assure your success in financial services!

Featuring the Legendary Skills and Experience of

Mehdi Fakharzadeh

Compiled by

Forrest Wallace Cato

Introduction by

Edwin P. Morrow

IARFC Press
"Helping you find and use the tools that work best for you"
2507 North Verity Parkway, Middletown, Ohio 45042-0430 USA
www.IARFC.org

Mehdi's *FAST-TRACK* Success System

Copyright © 2011 by Forrest Wallace Cato
Forrest Wallace Cato, 915 River Rock Drive, Suite 101, Woodstock, GA 30188-5338

ISBN 978-0-9828096-0-0

Library of Congress Control Number: 2010930573

All Rights Reserved

No part of this publication may be reproduced, stored in a retrieval system, or transmitted, in any form or by any means, electronic, mechanical, photocopying, recording, or otherwise, without the prior written permission of the publisher or the copyright holder.

Printed in the United States of America

… **Library of Congress Cataloging-In-Publication Data** …

File Under:
Insurance Sales, Financial Planning, Personal Financial Planning, Financial Plan, Investing, Estate Planning, Retirement Planning, Finances, Money, Wealth, Taxes, Life Insurance Agent, Financial Advisor, Financial Planner, Financial Consultant

Reference Under:
Financial Planning, Budgeting, Insurance, Insurance Needs, Annuities, Mutual Funds, Long Term Care, Portfolio Management, Trusts & Estates, Accounting, Fiduciary Responsibility, Economics, Money Management, Wealth Management

Authorized, Non-Abridged, Standard USA and International Edition

p.cm.
ISBN 978-0-9828096-0-0 (NON.LK. PAPER)
12 13 14 15 16 17 18 19 20

Permission for Quotation

Authors, editors and other publications may quote from this volume, with accreditation, limited amounts of text, defined as less than a full page. However this does not include multiple pages or forms, although such permission may be granted upon request.

For permission request, write to Intergroup II / Atlanta, Inc addressed "Attention Permission Coordinator" at the address indicated, or email to: **ForrestCato01@bellsouth.net** and please be specific about the extent of the material that is being requested for reproduction, and the nature of the publication in which it would be placed, such as a book, magazine, periodical, website, blog, CD-ROM or email.

Copyrights

All rights are hereby reserved under the **International Copyright Convention** as well as the **Pan-American Copyright Convention**. Except as permitted under the **United States Copyright Act of 1976**, no part of this volume may be reproduced, transmitted, or distributed in any form, or by any means, electronic or mechanical. This requirement includes photocopying, recording, or usage by any other information storage system(s), without the expressed permission, in writing, from the publisher.

Opinions and Positions

Views presented, indicated, or expressed herein, as well as opinions assumed or implied, may not necessarily be those of Mehdi Fakharzadeh, Forrest Wallace Cato, Edwin P. Morrow, or any other person or organization, indicated or not indicated herein. The views expressed within this volume or with the delivery, or the use of it in a classroom or internet setting, are those of the indicated writer or writers and not necessarily those of the International Association of Registered Financial Consultants or its separate members, the publisher, other writers, reviewers or endorsers, or other sources featured herein or referred to within the text. No legal or other affiliation, connection, involvement, or participation is suggested, implied, or alleged, regarding the sources mentioned herein.

Attempts have been made to insure accuracy of all the information and concepts presented in this volume, but the reader is hereby advised that financial planning techniques are highly determined by the investment, legal and regulatory situation – which is constantly under change. Where necessary the appropriate permissions have been sought and obtained from recognized owners of third party references and materials cited or used herein. No other representations are made or suggested with this publication. No obligations are assumed or implied pertaining to the individuals or institutions that may be referenced or mentioned as part of the use of this volume in classroom or Internet instruction.

Quantity Discounts

The publisher, IARFC Press, is willing to negotiate for the acquisition of large quantities of <u>Mehdi's Fast-Track Success System</u>, such as for distribution to a large segment of a sales force. It will also offer a quantity enrollment of students into the Fast-Track Workshop course, with classroom instruction to be offered in a location to be determined. Such circumstances might enable there to be special pricing opportunities for the course, instruction and materials, of which this volume is only one portion.

Related Websites and Email

Inquiries, comments and requests for updates, Fast-Track Workshops and presentations may be sent to:
www.CatoMakesYouFamous.com - Info@CatoMakesYouFamous.com
www.MehdiFast-Track.com - Info@MehdiFast-Track.com
www.IARFC.org - Editor@IARFC.org

Practice Compliance

Insurance agents and registered representatives may need to review the actions they take based on this Success System, such as the copy of mailings to prospects or clients. These may require submission for a compliance review. In general, Mehdi's Fast-Track Success System recommends the improvement of habits and attitudes, rather than specific practices or text, so action by the reader will not normally require any compliance submission

Instructional Usage

This work is suitable for use in a training or educational curriculum by educators and trainers. However, permission must be requested. The material may be used in part, or the publisher will consider a bulk sale of the work for use by a corporate training department or an educational institution.

Legal Advice

This publication is designed to provide accurate and authoritative information in regard to the subject matter covered. It is conveyed or sold with the understanding that the publisher and author(s) are not engaged in rendering legal, accounting, or other professional services. If legal advice or other expert assistance is required, the services of a competent professional person should be sought. The above is from a Declaration of Principles jointly adapted by a Committee of The American Bar Association and a Committee of Publishers and Associations.

Investment Advice

This publication is for use by persons that are or may become engaged in delivering general financial advice and financial products to consumers. It is not prepared for consumers, and there is no attempt to deliver investment advice, since the writers and publishers are not in the business of rendering such advice to consumers, and have not gathered all the personal information that would be necessary for the provision of such investment advisory services.

Limit of Liability Notice / Disclaimer of Warranty

While the publisher, editors(s), reviewers and related writers, have used their best efforts in preparing this book, they make no representations, or warranties, with respect to the accuracy, or completeness, of the contents of this book. These parties specifically disclaim any implied warranties, or endorsements, or suggestions of fitness for a particular purpose. Additionally, no warranty may be created or extended by instructors in a classroom or on the internet, or by sales representatives or by written sales materials.

The advice and strategies contained herein may not be suitable for any particular agent or financial advisor. The publisher is not engaged in rendering professional services directly to the consumer and each reader should consult additional professional counsel where appropriate. The publisher, editor(s), reviewers, or involved writer or writers, shall not be liable for any loss of profit or any other commercial damages, including but not limited to, special, incidental, consequential, or other damage or damages.

Manufacturing and Disposal Notes

This volume has been printed and assembled in the United States of America. It has been printed on acid-free and recycled paper composed of fifty percent or more of recovered fibers. This stock includes 10% post-consumer waste. Should the owner of this volume at some point wish to discard it, we encourage that the entire volume, including the cover, be placed in a "Recyclable" facility or container so that the materials can be reused, rather than contribute to the mountain of disposed and not re-used waste.

Table of Contents

Reviewer Comments vii
Comments by World Publishers xii
Introduction xiii
Acknowledgements xvii

A Personal Message from Mehdi 1

Why Mehdi is Important to You 3

How This Program Is Different For You … 5

Objectives of the *Fast-Track* System 7

Origin of the Fast-Track System 9

Mehdi Talks About Your System 11

Mehdi Explains *Fast-Track* Success 13

Let's Personalize Your Success System 17

Mehdi's Call to Action 21

My Personal Action Checklist 24

Mehdi's Success Tools 29

Career Profile - Mehdi Fakharzadeh 233

Career Profile - Forrest Wallace Cato 241

Career Profile - Edwin P. Morrow 249

About Your Image 255

Recommended Sources 257

𝑭𝑨𝑺𝑻-𝑻𝑹𝑨𝑪𝑲 Success Workshop 261

Experience Counts! 263

Information Opportunities 267

Reviewer Comments

Cato is the authorized biographer who completed an in-depth study of the unique life-long selling techniques and practices of MDRT hero Mehdi Fakharzadeh. This Success System documents **200 specific actions** you can take, or factors you can use, starting now, to highly improve your sales.
    Steve Forbes - Publisher

Mehdi is, without a doubt, one of the most cherished MDRT treasures since the organization was formed in 1927! His caring, and the sharing of his immense sales knowledge, makes him sought after all over the world! All our members know and respect Mehdi for his philosophy of putting service first.
    Guy E. Baker, CLU, ChFC, CFP, MSFS, MSM, RHU, CRWC - 2010 MDRT President, Author of *Why People Buy, Market Tune-Up, How I Made Top Of The Table 31 Times!*

Mehdi keeps everything simple, straightforward, and direct. He is always quick and to-the-point with his clients and his students. You can use Mehdi's Fast-Track Methods and raise your production to MDRT standards and beyond!
    Walton W. Rogers, CLU, ChFC - 2009 MDRT President

Mehdi turns every negative word or deed from others to an instant positive. He knows and practices the art of making others feel like royalty right now. He has given more than anybody I ever met – his attitude has made him a human being like none other!
    Alphonso Franco, RFC – Former MDRT TOT President

If I were a client of Mehdi, I would have bought with the first hug. His personal warmth allows you the opportunity to put aside your prejudices and listen to his message. The only mistake you could make – is not to listen to him.
    Stephen Rothschild, CLU, ChFC, RFC - 2006 MDRT President

Mehdi is without equal in his desire to share with all of us. He is a fountain of good habits and common sense. No one can read this book and not benefit.
    Van Mueller, LUTCF, RFC - Lecturer and Internet Publisher

There is nobody like Mehdi – in passing through this profession he has and will change many lives.
    Richard Sullenger - 2003 MDRT President

One of the icons of the profession in that you can always reach and talk with him, Mehdi will also share everything with you. He is the consummate sharer and mentor.
    Marvin Feldman, CLU, ChFC, RFC - 2002 MDRT President and TOT Chairman

Mehdi is simply the greatest, both as an insurance salesman, and more importantly, as a human being. His sales methods are simple and easily transferable to any market anywhere in the world. Any financial advisor who acquires Mehdi's fast-track skills and puts this system into practice will increase production, income, and success. If you adopt his caring and sharing attitude you will have a more fulfilling life.
    Tony Gordon - 2001 MDRT President

Mehdi is the only person in the world who insists that you go through the door before he does – and means it. It is impossible to have him precede you through an open door – because Mehdi always puts others first.
    Bruce Etherington, CLU, ChFC, CFP - Speaker and Author

The sales insights and guidance of The Great Mehdi enabled me to become the first woman in insurance history to go from sales agent to chairman of the board.
    LaNell Switzer, FIC

Mehdi is one of the greats of our profession. His integrity, foresight, and ability to meet the needs of his clients are second to none.
    Jack Peckinpaugh, CLU, RFC – Former NAIFA President

There is no better source for helping improve your insurance sales than that offered by the world's number one insurance sales agent. The entire curriculum of the Insurance Pro Shop® is built around what it took Mehdi a lifetime to learn and perfect. Many MDRT members owe Mehdi for sharing his knowledge.
    Irving Blackman, CPA, JD, RFC – Author of *Tax Secrets of the Wealthy*

I believe the greatest sales person of all time is Mehdi Fakharzadeh. The Great Mehdi is an MDRT leader because he is such a massively successful insurance agent. The sales world insists that Mehdi belongs to all of us, not only to financial advisors. Mehdi's techniques are *a* great gift to professionals who sell their services and sell big-ticket items or intangibles.
    Charles Tremendous Jones, RFC – Author of *People Are Tremendous (writing in 2008)*

With this system by the MDRT role model, you are holding a success system that can take you to greatness. I have personally been on many platforms with Mehdi and he is the best. You can be very busy, but only with the right sales system can you be highly productive.
    Garry Kinder, CLU, RFC, CSA - Author, Lecturer and Consultant

Mehdi is one of the great success stories in American history. A humble man with a service focus, an unrelenting work ethic and a commitment to his professional education were the traits that impressed me. I had the great fortune to meet him on several occasions early in my career with Metropolitan Life. Every insurance professional can learn from Mehdi regardless of where you are in your career.
    Edward Ledford, CLU, RFC - Foresters Financial Partners

Mehdi tells us about himself and his dedication to service, turning difficult needs into easy solutions. He shares everything about his life and his practice - with great openness.
    Benjawat Tantivongsakij, RFC – Former MDRT Zone Chair Thailand

Mehdi's advice and motivation has stimulated more average producers to become super achievers than all the financial sales gurus combined.
    George P. Brown, CLU, ChFC, RFC - Financial Advisor and estate planner

Shows you step-by-step how to custom tailor and use the one sales system that will work best for you.
    Timothy J. Haley, CPA/PFS, CFP, RFC - Advocate Financial Management

When you know exactly what you're trying to do, it is easier to figure out how to do it. Mehdi shows you exactly what to do to increase your sales.
Mickey M. Greenfield, JD, Ph.D., CAP, CPP – Author of *The Sales Slump Doctor Is In*

In this course, the wisdom, the experience, the history and even the genius of our greatest financial services sales elder is passed on to you.
T. Jerry Royer, FMM, RFC - Group 10 Financial

Access to the sales knowledge of Mehdi Fakharzadeh is an awesome privilege. He is a living legend in the insurance and financial planning worlds because he is one of the most successful producers. Though he is almost ninety years old, the Great Mehdi remains our leading sales powerhouse. He is also your truest source for learning how you can also become an insurance sales powerhouse!
Sandy Schussel, JD, RFC – Author of *Become a Client Magnet*

With a priority of always serving the best interest of my clients, I made half a million during my first year as a financial planner, a million during the second year, and over a million during my third year. The single most helpful factor in my success was the *Fast-Track* sales and service teachings of Mehdi Fakharzadeh. I am among those who love The Great Mehdi!
Phil Calandra, RFC - Tangibles specialist and MDRT member since 2006

Wait before you invest your money, time, and trust, in improving anything as important as your sales system. First make certain the sales system author knows how to sell. I've met the great MDRT hero, Mehdi Fakharzadeh, and financial sales people in England know that he is the highest producing sales professionals! People love this MDRT role model for the person he is and the way he sells. This is especially true of folks who use his proven sales system.
Rev. John Clements, Ph.D. – Author of *Make Your Walls Tumble*

In this one-of-a-kind course, the one true sales master shares his original proven techniques and his exclusive cutting-edge strategies that made him a world-wide sales phenomenon and consummate role model over the years. Now Mehdi enables other producers to catch the brass ring in the world of competitive selling. If you crave, greater sales success, then Mehdi's priceless system is your answer.
Jim McCarty, CLU, LUTCF, RHU, RFC – Author of *Showbiz Selling*

Mehdi said, "Of all the ways to make money, working as an insurance agent or financial planner is the highest paying hard work and the lowest paying easy work." He showed me the best actions to take so that my clients and I both win more. He helps you face your reality. He provides solutions with practicality. He suggests that nothing will be quick and easy. His advice and motivational values have stimulated average producers to become super achievers. Mehdi's Fast-Track Success System is worth every valuable second you invest. After you define your system – as Mehdi demonstrates – with diligent practice, you will become the leading financial representative in your market area.
Graceful Grady, CEA, WMS, RFC

Concentrate on what Mehdi Fakharzadeh teaches, then apply that which works best for you, and the impact will actually become a paradigm shift for you. He shows you how to become a trusted and appreciated advocate for your clients while zooming your sales and service.
Ugen Peden, RFC

The insurance learning curve I experienced required a long time. These years were full of constant twists and turns – a constant roller-coaster ride. I have wondered, since applying Mehdi's powerful insights, just how much shorter those trying years might have been, if I had been exposed to The Great Mehdi's guidance earlier in my career. We have all had thoughts from time-to-time about how the lack of certain exposures, or experiences, have hindered our advancements. Mehdi's system is your chance to avoid the difficult years and expedite your progress. The special answers that fit only your situation can all be found here. Now you can select and apply what you need, and you will reach the Top of the Table.
    Tony Brazeal, RFC - MDRT member since 1999

Mehdi's *Fast-Track* System is a must for every agent or planner who aspires to become a great financial professional. I have had the opportunity to see The Great Mehdi teach and train his unique system all over the world; in the USA, China, Singapore, and in other Pacific-Rim countries. Mehdi devoted his lifetime to creating this very effective system that you too can use to become an MDRT statesman.
    William L. Moore, CLU, ChFC, FIC, RFC - Kinder Brothers International, Co-Author of *Professional Patterns of Management* and *Dynamic Agency Management*

Here in Kuala Lumpur, Malaysia, you can ask most anyone in financial services, and they will likely tell you. The most brilliant sales mind in insurance sales is also the most brilliant sales agent on earth. And that is The Great Mehdi Fakharzadeh. We can all benefit from his extensive sales knowledge. He is our ultimate professional role model. His *Fast-Track* sales program is the most valuable sales system ever to benefit agents and planners.
    Jeffrey Chiew, ChFC, CFP, CLU, LUTCF, DBA, RFC - MDRT Chairperson, Malaysia
    Author, *The Art of Selling, How to Be A Super Achiever,* and *The Millionaire Formula*

The secrets of the MDRT's greatest hero -- the all-time sales record-making achiever often respectfully called, "The Great Mehdi" -- will be revealed when he codifies his powerful habits into a success system for agents and advisors. These will be the most helpful financial sales improvement methods of all time. Mehdi is possibly the most beloved guy in financial sales. He will definitely create the most effective sales system that you can use to speed your production to the highest level possible because that is precisely what he does for himself.
    Loren Dunton (1918-1997) (Writing in 1996) - Co-creator of the financial planning profession and founder of the IAFP, now the FPA and the College for Financial Planning

After 52-years in this business I thought I had seen it all, but the MDRT's legendary super-salesman, Mehdi Fakharzadeh has, over the years, developed a system that can place you on the *Fast-Track* to record personal production.
    Jack Gargan, CLU, RFC - Founder of IARFC and Author of *The Complete Guide To Estate Planning, How To Avoid Income Taxes, Milking Your Business For All Its Worth, How To Avoid Estate Taxes,* and *Money Management For Newlyweds And Other Beginners*

Mehdi is a priceless one-of-a-kind original! He is a treasure of both the MDRT and the IARFC. His focus on serving all persons, not just his clients, has elevated him to a height that is unique in financial services. The sales system and character that he embodies provide a priceless opportunity for you to serve far more clients and amass great wealth – all in record time.
    William J. Nelson, LUTCF, RFC - Director Learning Institute for Financial Executives and author of *Retirement Unlimited* and the *VUL Training Academy* textbooks

Mehdi Fakharzadeh is modest and makes no claim to fame or genius. But everyone well-knows he is simply one of the most successful insurance sales agents. Who among us could not learn from the master's *Fast Track Sales System?* Mehdi will always be a great hero.
>	**Brian Tracy** - International Speaker and Sales Trainer, Author of *Eat That Frog! The Art of Closing the Sale, Speak To Win, Goal Planner, The Psychology of Selling,* and *Success Is a Journey*

Mehdi's *Fast-Track* system utilizes blunt but practical and common sense language that enables virtually anyone to have the ability to sell more-and-more by using Mehdi's exclusive methods. He covers many new areas that have not already been well covered, or even revealed.
>	**Harold F. Chorney,** RTIA, RFC - President, Registered Tangibles Investment Advisors Association (RTIAA), Author of *What Happened To The Golden Frogs?*

This is the greatest sales improvement course ever! The Great Mehdi's *Fast-Track* Success System will accelerate you to a professional level of sales that you could only achieve through decades of hard work. Without his one-of-a-kind training you would spend years learning by experience. Mehdi Fakharzadeh is one of the most successful financial services salesmen of our time. But more importantly, Mehdi is truly a nice person. He has a history of always taking the time to help guide anyone who wants to highly improve their own sales. He spent two wonderful and priceless hours explaining to me, how I could be far more successful! I took notes like crazy! His methods worked, and continue to work, for me, for our team members.
>	**Stephen Bailey,** CEP, CSA, LUTCF, CEBA, MFP, RFC - President, IARFC and the author of *Dollar Sense: A Book For Mature Adults*

Financial professionals can now incorporate many of Mehdi's record-breaking sales ideas – those that you select as being most appropriate for your situation! With this *Fast-Track* help from The Great Mehdi, you can qualify for the MDRT and the IARFC.
>	**Vernon D. Gwynne,** CFP, RFC - Financial Planning Pioneer, IARFC Board Member, Former Executive Director of the IAFP, now the Financial Planning Association.

Only Mehdi's *Fast-Track* sales system® lays-out his practical steps to growing sales success in simple how-tos that you phrase in your own language. That aspect alone makes his teachings unique. But he synthesizes the wisdom of his decades of magnificent experience – all organized in clear language without gimmicks or embellishments. He breaks his proven selling process down into manageable steps – simple steps -- that new or experienced MDRT professionals can follow.
>	**Jeffrey Reeves** – Author of *Money for Life*

Many of Mehdi's tools can be used for more than one purpose. What at first may appear to be repetition (because the same tool is involved) is actually the application of that tool for another objective. Practice using the well-proven tools you select. Your chosen tools will become your winning habits. Your habits enable you to dominate your circumstances even during depression-like economic times.
>	**Geoffrey A. VanderPal** – CFP, CLU, CTP, MBA, RFC

Comments by World Publishers

"…the world's greatest financial sales system!" **Advisers magazine** (China)

"…the best financial sales and service system ever produced." ***The Register* magazine**

"The most effective financial product sales system yet devised." ***Financial Services Advisor* magazine**

"… the most useful financial sales program created to date." ***Fiduciary Legal Report***

"… by far the leading financial sales course of all time." ***Success Plans***

"Around the world, more successful agents and planners use Mehdi's financial sales system than most any other program." ***Popular Financing* magazine** (China)

"Practical tools of the revered grandfather of insurance and planning." ***Advisers magazine* (**Taiwan)

Introduction

This is not just another book written for agents and financial advisors!

Reading this book is potentially a *life changing event* because Mehdi encourages you to change your habits. Unlike encountering a valuable statistic, a new idea, or a colorful sales phrase - when you alter your habits you will make fundamental changes in your life!

While Mehdi is one of the world's greatest living life insurance salesmen, this is not a book about insurance. This book is about **Sales!**

Your Progress is Personal

You have grown, and you will continue to grow, both personally and professionally as a result of your personal effort and your personal changes. Others have influenced you positively in the past – and now you are about to be influenced personally by Mehdi Fakharzadeh.

Mehdi has evolved into the father figure for today's agents and planners. Doctors, lawyers, and other professionals work with a process using the elements that are most effective for their practices. Mehdi urges you to make more out of yourself by uncovering and using the process that works most effectively for you.

Everyone who is involved in marketing intangible products or services, especially in the financial field, will benefit from these tools. Just modify a few words and adopt the habits that Mehdi recommends. Do this and you will uncover the system that provides you with your most productive process.

This is a **System!** These Fast-Track tools will help you magnify the effectiveness of your professional career. But unlike many systems, this is not a linear progress. You should not try to adapt these new habits by going from #1 to #2 and on to #3. You should first extract from these tools those most critical to you and to your current situation.

This is a **Fast-Track** procedure – one designed to get immediate results for you. Mehdi encourages you to prepare your own Action Checklists – and as you extract and implement your most critical items, you'll feel a sense of accomplishment and achievement. This will reinforce your commitment to move on to additional tools.

Three Authors of this Success System

***Author #1* - Mehdi Fakharzadeh** – who is contributing the ideas, philosophies and techniques that have vaulted him to great success – as a salesman and as a human being.

***Author #2* - Forrest Wallace Cato** - who has transcribed and organized the incredible flow of ideas from Mehdi and arranged them in a consistent, logical fashion for your assimilation.

***Author #3* - You** – as you read each of these techniques you must cement your choices into your work habits and into your daily practice. Every day you can read one or two points, and take the essential step – to write down what you are going to do about this recommendation. How does it apply to your personal Success Fast-Track? What actions does this suggest that are appropriate for you?

When should you take action?

Immediately, of course! Let's say you decide to start using Mehdi's Success System this Sunday. Set aside two hours with no interruption. Have a tablet to make Action Step Notes for yourself. On this first day, your goal is to read the following portions:

- The initial pages of *Commentary* and the *Objectives of the Fast-Track Success System*. The objectives will instill you with enthusiasm and eagerness.

- The short chapter, *Mehdi Explains Fast-Track Success*, which takes you to the most important page.

- Mehdi has prepared you for stimulation with *Your Call to Action* and a sample checklist for your review.

- The first six or more items. Make written notes beneath Mehdi's observations. How does this apply to you? What can you implement immediately? Is there another resource you could use (a book, manual, webinar website, tape, etc.) and make notes to acquire it - or at least to gather more information?

- Transfer the Action Items to your note pad and vow to yourself that the following morning you'll move forward.

- Take action – Diligently follow-up on the items you placed on your personal Fast-Track Action Checklist.

- On the following day – set aside thirty minutes to review your comments and notes. How are you doing? Where do you need to concentrate more attention and energy?

- Next week. Review your progress and give yourself an evaluation using column 4. Return to this book and add new Fast-Track tools for your attention….. and continue to repeat this process. You will be forming and strengthening your **Habits for Greater Success.**

Please make note of the last items in this manual. Would your agency, company or professional association be interested in hosting a ***Fast-Track* Workshop** that would guide the attendees through understanding and getting started on improving their sales habits?

Would an organization with which you are associated (insurance company, broker/dealer, bank, etc.) benefit from a speaker – on Mehdi's *Fast-Track* Success System, or another related topic.

Would you like to receive updates and information?

If so, simply complete the form on the very last page, and send it in.

Edwin P. Morrow, CLU, ChFC, CEP, CFP, RFC
Chairman, International Association of Registered Financial Consultants

Acknowledgements

Every major published work reflects input from supporters and contributors. It is difficult to measure the extent of these valuable additions. The true beneficiary of their contributions to this book is you - because you receive a more complete publication as a result of the following persons:

Sigrun Fakharzadeh – Wife of Mehdi Fakharzadeh

Kimberly A. McCoy – Mehdi's assistant at the Wealth Financial Group, MetLife

Wajma Ahmad – Mehdi's assistant at the Wealth Financial Group, MetLife

Tony Gordon – past president of MDRT

John J. Prast - MDRT Executive Vice President

Stephen P. Stahr - MDRT Managing Director

Jennifer Schimka - MDRT Media Relations Coordinator

Gina Fadin - MDRT Executive Assistant

Kathryn F. Keuneke - MDRT Editor of *Round the Table* magazine

Colleen Schneider - MDRT Program Assistant

Chester Chu - MDRT Chair for Asia Pacific

Matteo Pederzoli - MDRT Regional Director for Europe

Sandra Dees – Executive Assistant, Intergroup II / Atlanta, Inc.

Mark Terrett – Operations Manager for the IARFC

Amy Primeau – Domestic Member Services for the IARFC

Wendy M. Kennedy – Editor of the *Register* magazine, published by the IARFC

Jim Lifter – Director of Education for the IARFC

Liang Tien Lung – IMM International, Worldwide Chinese Life Insurance Congress

Wu Chin-Chu & Wang Ting-Chi - Nothing is Impossible, Everything is Possible

Mark Patterson – For his development of the cover of this book

Norman G. Levine – association executive, sales leader, pioneer and a veteran contributor to the financial services and life insurance professions

It has been said that:

**All Development is
Personal Development!**

This work is dedicated to the millions of
agents, advisors, planners and brokers
who serve individuals, families and small
businesses with integrity and enthusiasm.

A Personal Message from Mehdi

You are different from all other financial services practitioners. You have unique abilities and individual strengths. The world's most successful insurance agents and financial planners all use a sales system that is carefully structured especially for them.

Their systems are tailored to take advantage of their unique strengths. A customized and personalized sales success system is proven to produce the best results.

Unfortunately, some agents and financial advisors use a system that actually works against them. Why would anyone actually support a system that works against them?

Failure is certain if you use no system at all. Limited sales results are assured by using a sales system that is wrong for you. Using the wrong sales system (that does not work well for you), makes your life and your sales far more difficult.

Only the sales system that is just right for you will enable you to take control of your time. Only your carefully tailored sales system will enable you to become productive to your maximum potential! This program will guide you in selecting the tailored-for-you sales system that will work best for you.

Mehdi Fakharzadeh, MS, CLTC, RFC

It has been said that:

**_Leaders Always Lead By
Encouraging Others Onward!_**

We hope that you will encourage others
to employ the principles of this work –
and to participate actively in one or more
professional societies, like MDRT, IARFC,
SFSP, NAIFA, FPA and many others.

Why Mehdi is Important to You

Mehdi Fakharzadeh, RFC, is a life insurance sales agent. He is also one of the most successful living insurance sales agents in the world!

Mehdi's entire career is based on simple, but powerful beliefs – and the habits he has developed to perform them on a daily basis. Mehdi is convinced that **Great Habits Produce Sales Success!**

But he is regarded by his clients as more of a financial service professional, than simply someone selling products! His clients often refer to him as "Mister Mehdi" and that respect has enabled him to achieve and hold his great reputation, world-wide.

This sales master is also a master sales teacher. He is both a recognized and honored hero and role model to the MDRT, IARFC and NAIFA organizations.

This one-of-a-kind sales legend has been the centerpiece of many articles that revealed his techniques. They have also featured his personal commitment – that a life of financial sales is really a life of service….

In Asia, where he has lectured over a hundred times, he is often called "The Great Mehdi" simply because he is beloved world-wide for his tireless efforts to share his unique sales knowledge and special skills.

Mister Mehdi is important to you because he can help you establish your own unique and individualized sales system -- the one system that will work best for you, and maximize your sales.

You can maximize your sales, starting now.

How This Program Is Different For You …

The objective of this system is not an attempt to make you into a duplicate of Mehdi. Our goal is to build onto your uniqueness and make you more powerful and effective as the special individual that you are. Our goal is also to enhance your strengths while stabilizing your abilities.

This is accomplished by enabling you to identify and define –

> *in your own words, not in our terms, the precise elements you need to compose the sales Success System most effective for you.*

This system requires that you highly influence the development of your own habits and that you use love (for compassion, patience, understanding, and consideration) in dealing with your prospects and clients.

Mehdi Fakharzadeh doesn't teach the quarterback how to catch. He shows you how to work on what works best for you.

Once you complete this program and apply your tailored system in your marketplace for a few months, you will instinctively know that you can hugely improve your productivity. Many professional people in financial products and services use Mehdi's methods to get on a faster-track and become top world-class producers.

Once you know **what to do**,

> **and believe**,
>
> **then you will achieve**
>
> **the success you deserve!**

Objectives of the *Fast-Track* System

- Select, customize, and use, the sales system that works best for you.
- Love and care about your prospects and your clients.
- Assemble and use the tools you need to sell at your best.
- Replace defective and depressing habits with productive habits
- Arrange your sales efforts and keep them organized.
- Control your sales efforts to keep them highly productive.
- Get maximum productive use of your time and find more time.
- Become a generator of ideas, actions, procedures, and events.
- Obtain leads, evaluate your prospects, and identify decision makers.
- Discover how the decision maker's process works.
- Meet and greet effectively, pre-plan, make better presentations.
- Close and follow-up consistently, to better serve your clients.
- Gain and use your product benefit knowledge.
- Track your prospecting and client service using a CRM program.
- Master effective ways for you to "break the ice."
- Figure out what your prospect's real issues are.
- Establish rapport and always build trust.
- Control your sales call (and overall sales efforts) at all stages.
- Continue your process of learning and improving.
- Tap the resources of professional organizations
- Build interest in you by improving your image.
- Consider the impact of using an image consultant.
- Be ready to overcome the most encountered selling obstacles.
- Avoid the most common sales mistakes.
- Partner to create a mutual win-win situation.
- Stick with the tried-and-true steps and procedures.
- Maintain your motivation despite set-backs.
- Manage rejections and disappointments.
- Use proven systems to maximize your approach to new prospects.

- Protect yourself from sales burnout and emotional depletion.
- Know when to use your good judgment or common sense.
- Build and maintain your morale and sense of self-worth.
- Remain focused on what is important to move you to your next level.
- Retain your enthusiasm and find joy in your daily work.
- Make self-attitude adjustments when necessary.
- Find more leads and qualify your leads.
- Learn ways to gather information about your most logical prospects.
- Revise elements of your *Fast-Track* system when necessary.
- Master effective ways to handle rejections.
- Learn how to communicate with unresponsive people.
- Make every call a personal call and a proper sales call.
- Reach an agreement and close a deal.
- Help set goals for your clients.
- Set and achieve your sales goals.
- Consider the value and image impact of charging a fee.
- Manage your valuable time so you do not waste time.
- Evaluate your performance.
- Use New Client Revenue (NCR) to justify all of your marketing efforts.
- Encourage you to be active in one or more professional associations.
- Use tested and proven sources to accelerate your transformation.
- Keep your selling efforts a growth process.
- Dialogue to build trust and relationships.
- Know what to do when a prospect refuses to meet with you.
- Deal with the prospect's fear, laziness, or ignorance.
- Uncover your prospect's agenda.
- Plant seeds, and leave "footprints," and "triggers."
- Gather appropriate information to help you sell.
- Do pre-call planning to improve your odds for success.
- Use agendas and pre-formatted notes to impress prospects and clients
- Consider the 200 dynamic tools and other ideas stimulated by this system.
- Become a highly successful insurance agent or financial planner.

Origin of the *Fast-Track* System

Mehdi has presented his Fast-Track Success System briefings to eager insurance agents, financial planners, and money advisors, in over thirty-three countries.

- This course originated as a one-of-a-kind quick briefing, composed of elements presented in no logical order.

- This material kept expanding until becoming a full program, and eventually a complete course evolved.

- The various combined financial professionals who understood, adopted, and used "the portions they selected as right for them" from among **Mehdi's Methods**, went on to experience significant increases in their sales and service results.

- Most of these sales increases were documented. The total amount from these improved sales, while not precisely calculated and totaled, have now reached multi-million dollar figures!

The brief capsule explanations of his unique and original methods, over time, grew into "Mehdi's Fast-Track Sales System – a complete program containing 270 proven dynamics that is usually presented to small standing-room-only groups.

- Individual discussion is planned into this learning experience.

- These select gatherings have become near legendary among sales trainers and within the insurance world.

- The impact of these teaching techniques has resulted in significantly increased sales production.

With this in mind, we asked Mehdi to present, in his own words, his original system here for you, and we recorded the instructions which follow. The format in which this content is presented is designed to encourage the reader and the workshop participant to focus on the methods that are likely to be most effective for him or her.

Compiling Years of Success

As Mehdi Fakharzadeh's biographer, and also a long-time friend of the famous sales master, I must confess my amazement:

> *Of all the great sales people I ever interviewed, or met; as the Editor-in-Chief of two of the leading financial magazines, only Mister Mehdi is very*

concerned about the sales results of others. He often works to help increase their sales totals.

He actually wants others to surpass his sales achievements. He would actually be delighted if one of the readers broke his long-standing sales records. This sales genius truly wants you to exceed his record-breaking sales accomplishments.

Notice the many ways – over the years -- in which 'Mister Mehdi' strived to help others accomplish their sales objectives. He believes that he has been blessed and he wants to share everything he knows with others who serve the public. He is thrilled to watch his students climb their own ladders of success. He feels they are all part of a brotherhood that he is obligated to help.

Again we repeat: "Mister Mehdi" has conducted this Fast-Track Sales Course to limited groups of sales people around our globe.

In various countries, many of those who participated in this exclusive program went on to qualify for MDRT and/or RFC status, and became world-class sales and service achievers.

We commissioned "Mister Mehdi" with the following four-point challenge:

- Could you please tell us everything – everything that you reveal in your famous fast-track programs – once again?

- Please include anything and everything that you use -- to become and remain extremely successful -- even if you only seldom use something.

- Can you please deliver your unique wisdom again, by once more presenting your methods that are proven to fast-track insurance agents and financial planners to greater heights of sales achievements?

- Will you please present this using your "uncover the best answers yourself" method that enables the participant to figure out his or her own solutions that will work best?"

As you use this system to form new and better habits, continue to remind yourself that other agents and advisors just like you have used Mehdi's Fast-Track Tools to achieve success.

If they can, you can...!

Mehdi Talks About Your System

Throughout our world, especially during these tough economic times, most people do not fulfill their potential. This is especially true of insurance agents and financial planners. Why is this?

- Selling is very difficult - even miserable - without the most effective sales system.

- Professionals who must sell their services, but fail to adequately sell, are not weak people. Just as salesmen who fail are not bad people.

- The proper and essential dynamics must be in alignment for top results.

Your sales are not produced by memorizing clichés, threatening, punishing, management quotas, prizes, deadlines, reducing costs, rewards, trophies, demanding, gimmicks, etc.

Great sales will be produced by your discovering the best combination of individual sales dynamics. Within this book I've listed 200 of the dynamics I have used in my personal Success System.

What you must do is to employ them to form the sales system that works most effectively for you, and then polish your system through repeated use (practice).

The system you create for yourself will be your system, not mine! The effective sales system you use will be composed mostly of dynamics that I have asked you to consider, and from which you will carefully make selections. These selections are priceless investments in you and your future.

At any point in time your financial status is determined by your choices that become your habits. My system will help you focus on the many actual additional choices that you have – choices of which you may not have been aware.

Even your attitude is your choice. You do not have to be squeezed and molded so that you can be used and exploited. Your own 'results-producing system' frees you, stimulates your thinking abilities, and assures your confidence.

The only difference between financial advisors who are highly successful and those who are only average lies in the differences in their habits. Your sales system makes the difference in your habits. Your winning sales system empowers you with what you need and can do the best.

If you maintain your motivation and discipline, then nothing can prevent you from achieving your sales goals, once you define and use the right system for you.

When you are "locked" into your own proven system, you can then "bounce back" as necessary. You know in advance that you can overcome any obstacle because you are aware that your success is the sum of your habits.

Most of your habits are small efforts repeated day-after-day.

Your customized system helps you always to make the most valuable use of your time as you stay focused and highly productive. The right system for you allows you time for life's other essentials. You cannot hope to participate fully in maximum sales without using the system that is just right for your individual situation and circumstances. Your system keeps you strongly in command.

Mehdi Fakharzadeh, MS, CLTC, RFC

Mehdi Explains *Fast-Track* Success

This ***Fast-Track*** **Success System** has grown over the years from 42 to 200 dynamic tools. They have gradually evolved as I shared my career history with audiences in over 50 countries. Again and again, producers kept asking me not to leave the stage. They did not want me to stop talking about how to improve their selling results with my basic, non-technical methods.

Those present wanted more. Certain audience members insisted that I could provide them with more useful knowledge! They claimed that I was not revealing everything that I did. And they specifically wanted <u>all</u> of my key methods, each summarized in simple words. They wanted this condensed and clear.

> **However, in most sales conferences the attendees have nothing on which to write. As a result, valuable ideas are rarely acted upon by the attendees.**

Some in financial services are successful because of their connections, their intellect, or their ability to seize some trend at just the right time.

> **My personal success has come from <u>habits.</u> I firmly believe the *Fast-Track* methods for most persons lie in forming <u>better habits</u>.**

My audiences contained fans and admirers who wanted me to cover everything, rather than explain only certain topics. So I began to expand my briefings, trying to cover additional aspects - as much as can be possible. I found it impossible to prioritize the elements involved, so I went back to listing them in no specific order.

Eventually I had a program, which grew into this ***Fast-Track*** Success System – which can be used as a standalone manual or as part of a course. The random order in which the tools are presented is also by design - as I feel that all course participants must learn better to multi-task mentally, be flexible in their routines, and work with some contradictory and subjective guidelines.

Over the years I continually edited my material for brevity. I realized that financial product and service representatives learned faster, did better, and benefited more, if they were not spoon-fed by me or by anyone else.

> **Most of my "students" later achieved increased production if I presented this material in a format where they were told what to solve, and then left to their own resources for finding the solutions that work best for them.**

So my sales improvement course is different from all other sales training because the *Fast-Track* **Success System** is designed to encourage you to search for, and find, the answers that work best for you.

Where necessary I also give you a clue or two to help you figure out how to resolve a situation or circumstance successfully.

I believe that when you dig out the helpful information you need you will be more likely to remember and act upon the information you uncover. You will be more inclined to continually use this information, especially when you start realizing the increased benefits to you.

> **The resulting information you get is always what I intended for you. Your guides and plans will be framed by your thoughts and not by the dictates of my words.**

You will focus on your own solutions, using your own terms. Some repetition is intentionally included for emphasis.

Most agents and planners have been spoon fed sales techniques, strategies, or concepts - and then forgotten them or devalued them in their later thoughts and experiences.

Throughout history, in every land and in every industry, the most powerful ideas and tools are rather simple when viewed with perspective.

Starting at this moment, you can be like Sherlock Holmes and solve the mysteries of what you need to do to improve your sales results if I present you with the likely puzzle elements and some target clues.

Don't forget to consult *Recommended Sources* at the end of this work.

> **Master the fundamentals of this *Fast-Track* Success System and you can place the portions of my methods that work best for you into actions for your sales benefit.**
>
> **And you can do so immediately!**

Fast-Track Formatting

Every reader has purchased textbooks on sales and marketing, and on how to sell complex policies or create convoluted comprehensive plans. Most of these books are 400-500 pages long, and the layouts make it difficult to determine what to do next.

Therefore, each nugget containing a success habit that can improve your career is presented just one to a page. Below each item is lots of space for you to write – while you are reading each for the first time.

This is an important aspect of gaining maximum value from the *Fast-Track* Success Course. What should you write on these pages?

- Your personal reactions to an item

- How applicable is this suggestion to you?

- Should you do any special research?

- Do you need additional resources?

- Is this an action for tomorrow or next month?

Let's Personalize Your Success System

Remember, I have said, great results will come to you, not from technical items or presentation tools, however valuable they might be!

***Your Habits Will Make You
Or Your Habits Will Break You***

Much of what I have learned I acquired not only from my personal experience (and I've had a lifetime of trials and errors in the world of selling financial products and services) but also from the world's great insurance agents, financial planners, sales trainers, motivators, and self-help writers.

These same sources have always been equally available to you. I'm talking about people like Ed Morrow, Ben Feldman, Guy Baker, Tony Gordon, Norman Vincent Peale, Norman G. Levine, Robert H. Schuller, Dale Carnegie, Walton W. Rogers, and many other wonderful people.

My friend, Forrest Wallace Cato, the American media advocate for financial professionals, wrote a best-selling book in China, the main point of which is, you become successful according to what you do by habit. Cato believes your habits lead you directly to where you are, be that success, failure, mediocrity, or something else. I too believe this because my experience and my system prove this to be true.

As you go through my *FAST-TRACK* **Success System** I will be trying to get you to select, customize and implement new sales habits of your own. You will notice that I am always attempting to influence your habits.

**The more productive habits you adopt from this course,
the more successful you will become.**

Everything I have accomplished I owe to the habits I developed and practiced over and over through my life. Over time I revised and refined my habits. I discontinued some habits, and I added new ones to my repertoire.

My sales, work, conduct, operation, and life-style habits took me straight to universal record-breaking sales achievements. Certainly the habits you make can make you what you want to be.

You must stay focused on your most productive habits and always adhere to them. Do this and your advancements will be certain!

You may be asking yourself, "Why is Mehdi focusing on habits, when what I want is just a simple way to close the big case, or acquire more clients?"

Proper habits place you on the correct track. Without proper habits you may not even be on the road to your success. Without the proper habits you may never even have the opportunity to present that big case. My system, when adequately utilized, places you on the express lane to maximizing your success.

Most people in financial sales and service, or in any other profession, do not absolutely stick with proven success habits. Instead most people "do anything" or "whatever" from day to day, depending on the "various circumstances that take place mostly by accident." Doing this is a "no-no."

> **Starting immediately, your permanent priority is creating, practicing, and remaining loyal to specific enduring and positive habits that will move you along the track to your greater success.**

Please Follow These Instructions

From among the items I am about to present here, in this *Fast-Track* **Success System**, you can pick and choose those areas that you feel will be most important for you.

You do not have to master every item that this course will help you uncover and realize. In fact, it would be impossible to achieve full mastery within a year. But the more you master, the greater your increased production results will be – and this will increase your concentration on better habits, eventually empowering you.

1. **Circle or mark the items you believe will help you most. These represent the areas which you recognize should be mastered first.**

2. **After you have circled all of the items you want to adopt first, go through those items again. This time, rank them in the order that you would like to accomplish them.**

3. **After you have these dynamics arranged in the order to be accomplished, you can now determine the correct actions necessary to master each of them.**

4. **These necessary actions will reveal to you the habits you must adopt and honor for the rest of your productive life.**

5. **If you need additional help, then consult the Recommended Sources section at the end of this volume.**

Even a Poor Start is Better than No Start

Do this! Start now! Begin immediately to form and follow these habits and your greater success and advancement will actually be assured. Of course, this is all much easier said than done. But this is well-proven to be very doable. You can do this if you are determined.

You will do this if you are determined to become as successful as you can be. These habits will help you form a winner's mindset that will enable you to execute additional actions that will allow you to take on still more, different, and other, tasks and projects. This, in turn, will lead you to acquiring additional credits, status symbols, prestige, special achievements, tools, and related accomplishments, all by and for you.

> **This is a realistic, practical, understandable, and dependable formula for your greater success. If executed with precision you cannot fail.**

I was not born with massive talents. I am not a genius of any type. I was simply lucky. Why lucky? I was lucky because I realized one truth:

> **I eventually realized this *Fast-Track* Success Course is one that never fails - and I use this System myself, on a daily basis.**

If you devote yourself to using the parts of this system that work best for you, then nothing can stop you from moving up, and up, and up, and up! The *Fast-Track* Success System will empower you.

Now – Get Started!

These dynamic Success Tools are the areas which can help you.

- If you like, you can start now to circle the areas that you feel you most need to master or upon which you seek improvement.

- Some readers may prefer to read each item a second time and then enter their notes or action steps.

- After you determine what actions to take to master your circled subjects, only then can you determine the habits to form and practice.

Soon it will become clear to you: There are many dynamic Success Tools that apply to you – so many, in fact, that you must prioritize them, and only work at a limited number at a time.

Your resulting and practiced habits will advance you to far greater success – starting when you do.

To help you I have created a form for you to use in developing and using your personal, *FAST-TRACK* Action Checklist.

Mehdi's Call to Action

Creating Your *Fast-Track* Action Checklists

On the following pages are blank *Fast-Track* Success Checklists for you to reproduce and use. I realize it would be impossible for you to take action on each of these items each day.

- Good habits are hard to form – time is required. Weeks or months may be needed.

- Bad habits are even harder to break – this takes determination.

I want you to do what I did when I got my career moving. I focused on a limited number of items every week and I kept reminding myself about what I was to work on improving. Did I succeed every week – of course not! Often I had to work on a Success Habit for more than a month. But I was persistent, and that really paid off.

Don't Waste Your Time or Money

The greatest system in the world is useless – unless you implement that system. All you will achieve with these proven Success System Tools – is to waste a bit of money on this guide and your reading time – unless you firmly and resolutely take action!

Remember, "All Development is Self-Development." Take action!

How to Use Your Personalized Checklists

The important thing is to keep your personalized checklist "in your face" so that you will be constantly aware of the habits you want to change or adopt.

If you want to print your personalized checklists with your computer, we would be pleased to send you the file by email – send your request to:

Info@MehdiFast-Track.com

However, what you might find easier is carefully removing one of the blank checklist pages, make photocopies and make your entries by hand.

Keep Reminding Yourself

You can use a *Checklist Display Stand* as a reminder.

You can purchase an excellent slanted sign holder that is sized for 8.5" by 11" paper. Many sales professionals use this type of stand to place a script in front of a sales associate who is making calls. But, if you purchase one or two, you can insert your current *Personalized Fast-Track Checklist* in the stand, and place it (ideally) between your phone and your computer.

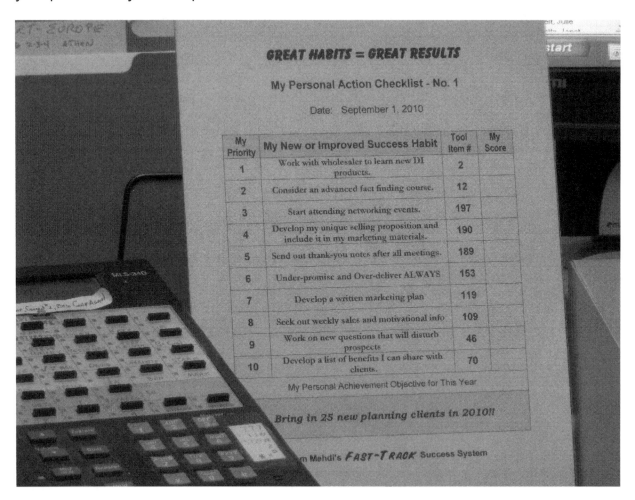

Soon you will learn to review your checklist quickly, and then take action to strengthen the habits you are focusing on that week. Remember, what we have been saying: **Better Habits Produce Greater Sales!**

Start by Completing Checklist #1

Your checklist may contain what you consider your "Top 10" Action Items. The number is not important – you might list 12 items, or only 6.

As you master some habits, you will have the opportunity to applaud yourself by removing them from your daily viewing. You will be on the road to success, because you are forming positive permanent habits.

- Review the *Sample Checklist* on the next page.

- Prepare your initial action checklist

- Every week, score your performance (1 = low to 10 = high)

- Prepare a new checklist for next week, and add some items.

- Save your old checklists; periodically review them and add items that were there before back to the list if necessary.

GREAT HABITS = GREAT RESULTS

My Personal Action Checklist - No. 1

Date: September 1, 2010

My Priority	My New or Improved Success Habit	Tool Item #	My Score
1	Work with wholesaler to learn new DI products.	2	
2	Consider an advanced fact finding course.	12	
3	Start attending networking events.	197	
4	Develop my unique selling proposition and include it in my marketing materials.	190	
5	Send out thank-you notes after all meetings.	189	
6	Under-promise and Over-deliver ALWAYS	153	
7	Develop a written marketing plan	119	
8	Seek out weekly sales and motivational info	109	
9	Work on new questions that will disturb prospects	46	
10	Develop a list of benefits I can share with clients.	70	
	My Personal Achievement Objective for This Year		
	Bring in 25 new planning clients in 2010!!		

From Mehdi's *FAST-TRACK* Success System
Copyright © 2011 – All Rights Reserved

GREAT HABITS = GREAT RESULTS

My Personal Action Checklist - No. ___

Date: _____

My Priority	My New or Improved Success Habit	Tool Item #	My Score
1			
2			
3			
4			
5			
6			
7			
8			
9			
10			

My Personal Achievement Objective for This Year

Enter Your Most Important Goal for the Year Here

From Mehdi's **FAST-TRACK** Success System
Copyright © 2011 – All Rights Reserved

GREAT HABITS = GREAT RESULTS

My Personal Action Checklist - No. ____

Date: _____

My Priority	My New or Improved Success Habit	Tool Item #	My Score
1			
2			
3			
4			
5			
6			
7			
8			
9			
10			
	My Personal Achievement Objective for This Year		
	Enter Your Most Important Goal for the Year Here		

From Mehdi's *FAST-TRACK* Success System
Copyright © 2011 – All Rights Reserved

GREAT HABITS = GREAT RESULTS

My Personal Action Checklist - No. ___

Date: _____

My Priority	My New or Improved Success Habit	Tool Item #	My Score
1			
2			
3			
4			
5			
6			
7			
8			
9			
10			
	My Personal Achievement Objective for This Year		
	Enter Your Most Important Goal for the Year Here		

From Mehdi's *FAST-TRACK* Success System
Copyright © 2011 – All Rights Reserved

GREAT HABITS = GREAT RESULTS

My Personal Action Checklist - No. ___

Date: _____

My Priority	My New or Improved Success Habit	Tool Item #	My Score
1			
2			
3			
4			
5			
6			
7			
8			
9			
10			
	My Personal Achievement Objective for This Year		
	Enter Your Most Important Goal for the Year Here		

From Mehdi's FAST-TRACK Success System
Copyright © 2011 – All Rights Reserved

Mehdi's Success Tools

Mehdi's Success Tool # 1

Selling financial products or services is informing, educating, and motivating your prospect to take action in his or her best interest, by purchasing, investing, and planning.

Your selling is not forceful persuasion. Your selling is intelligent reason and logic, presented respectfully, to bring about understanding and agreement.

Can you learn how to motivate with practical truths that embody obvious reason and logic? How? What could you do to accomplish this? That is your first mystery.

Act like Sherlock Holmes and uncover the ways you can motivate with practical truths that embody obvious reason and logic.

Enter Your Responses and Personal Action Steps

Mehdi's Success Tool # 2

I have made, and continue to make, many sales simply because I have product benefit knowledge. These sales were 'given to me.' I did not have to work hard for these sales. Often little work was involved. Some people, when they agree to see you, are already interested and they simply want accurate and complete product knowledge. **Can you acquire and maintain accurate and complete product knowledge that is always up-to-date?**

This becomes a part of your specialty knowledge. This helps make you valuable to your clients and prospects. Never attempt to fake product knowledge. I have known many salespeople who faked product knowledge or had only limited knowledge. But, I have never known a top producer who lacked complete product knowledge.

Enter Your Responses and Action Steps

Mehdi's Success Tool # 3

Look for winners. Winners are always doers and strivers! Seek out achievers! Search for competent and productive people. Target intelligent, thoughtful, high-class people who are active, involved, lead useful, passionate lives, and are very busy. (This describes all of my clients.)

You don't have to target only wealthy prospects. But you are not likely to sell to a homeless person, a prisoner, a drifter, an unreliable or irresponsible individual, a wasted drug addict, or to a person who deserts his family. Your best prospect is …

- A person that cares, reasons, and thinks
- A person who resides in a well-maintained house
- A person who keeps his car clean and well-running
- A person who is neat, clean, with a good haircut or hair style
- A person displaying shined or clean footwear
- Someone wearing tasteful jewelry
- A person with good teeth and breath
- A person who is articulate and attentive
- A person who has a sharp and orderly appearance
- A person who collects walking sticks or stamps
- A person with a passion for studying ancient history
- A person who is always building a personal library

Can you identify people (they give-off little clues) who are not appropriate prospects for you? Can you list some characteristics of both types – those who are most likely to be good prospects, and those who are not likely to do substantial business, with you?

Identify your best prospects, based on your history and on your judgment. Can you identify the **best characteristics** to seek in your prospects – and **characteristics in people you should avoid?** Remember, these factors are subjective and should be based on your desired target market!

Characteristics of Your Best Prospects

Characteristics of Your Worst Prospects

Mehdi's Success Tool # 4

"Loser" types will not buy from you - nor from anyone else. These unfortunate people often need different types of help and assistance to adequately survive. They often go from crisis-to-crisis.

"Winner" types will understand your offer, appreciate the benefits, and they will buy from you. Winner types are more consistent and stable.

What are the points I have just made? Why is this important for you?

Enter Your Responses and Action Steps Below

Mehdi's Success Tool # 5

Most financial specialists will immediately answer every question even when they do **not** know the correct answer. This is a terrible practice! Such advisors may feel they must present an impression of knowing everything. Or, they may view 'not being able to answer' as a weakness. So they fake answers. They may believe not answering reveals poor product knowledge. Often they almost answer, or answer something else, change the subject, or ignore the question.

But, a true expert or authority can easily say "I don't know." Doing so does not cause you to lose face or cause you to lose the confidence of your prospect. Doing so increases your prospect's respect and trust for you - as long as you do not say this too often. You can always say "I will research this for the best answer and get back to you." If necessary, for a limited number of times per prospect, you can say, "I don't know." Then indicate that you will research or make special efforts to find correct answers.

Can you do this - and prompt yourself to get back on a timely basis?

Enter Your Responses and Your Follow-up Action Steps

Mehdi's Success Tool # 6

Far too many salespeople, at every level of selling, (whether selling products, ideas, or services) tell large or small lies (untruths) to make a sale.

These people give selling a bad name. They are also unsuccessful in the long run. They make selling more difficult for all of the honest sales professionals. They will promise almost anything, embellish, mislead, or withhold key information. In our profession they are known as "Clowns!"

How can you find and keep the courage and strength to be honest? How can you assure yourself that you will never say or do anything dishonest even though you think it will help you close the sale?

Enter Your Responses and Action Steps

Mehdi's Success Tool # 7

Salespeople, at all levels, are often accused of taking advantage of other people's problems, needs, insecurities, fears, sorrows, concerns, etc. Some salespeople do this. They too give selling a negative reputation and make work more difficult for honest sales professionals. This is not acceptable.

But it is acceptable to adapt your approach and interaction according to your target prospect's problems, needs, insecurities, fears, sorrow, concerns, etc. You do this largely when you take ownership of their concerns or issues.

Can you explain these right and wrong differences? Taking ownership of your prospect's issues is the only logical course if you are truly going to serve your prospect's best interest. **Why is "doing the right thing" important for you?**

Enter Your Responses and Action Steps

Mehdi's Success Tool # 8

You absolutely must take "ownership" of your prospect's issues and concerns. This starts with probing questions that are not judgmental. It is also very effective to repeat and clarify the prospect's important positions.

Can you do this in a tactful and thorough fashion?

What related practices do you have that you should avoid?

What practices do you have now that you could strengthen, or use more often, to achieve the correct image with your clients? **How can you remind yourself to do this in every interview?**

Enter Your Responses and Action Steps

Mehdi's Success Tool # 9

If you find that your competition "looks better" than you, then your competition will most likely "sell better" than you.

If this is the case, then your competition will appear to be sharper and serve more people than you.

Your smartest competition will present the image of being more successful, and will try to use this image to put you at a disadvantage!

How can you prevent this?

Explain Your Responses and Planned Actions

Mehdi's Success Tool # 10

You must always dress as a professional should dress! This includes your grooming – haircut or styling, your fingernails, etc.

But, how can you do this effectively?

Answer: You must wear a neat, dignified, suit, shirt, and tie, with shined shoes, knee-length black socks, neat haircut, and appropriate jewelry accessories, including your belt buckle, briefcase, laptop computer pouch, notebook, and writing instruments. Everything you have with you must pass this test, including your hair styling, sunglasses, a tie bar or tie chain, cufflinks, lapel pin, etc.

A female financial professional should wear her version of appropriate business attire and accessories. For example, nails should be neat and subtle. Excessive jewelry is a distraction and to some prospects will imply that "trendy fashion" is more important than client service.

Careful dress reflects courtesy. So does noticeably turning off your cell phone, implying that your full attention is devoted to your prospect or client.

Enter Action Steps to Enhance Your Image

Mehdi's Success Tool # 11

During some occasions you may call on a prospect and almost immediately you will sense this prospect is being difficult, unpleasant, obstinate, or even rude. What do you do in this situation?

Answer: Rather than rush through as much of your routine as possible, try to force yourself to do just what you would do with a nicer or typical prospect. At the least this can be an experience that helps you refine your skills and build your discipline.

Slow down, be attentive and have warm eye contact. Your prospect may be nervous or distracted by some non-related issue.

As part of your persistence habit, remember to follow-up on this prospect. After all, it is possible that this prospect was just having a bad day. If the prospect is a total curmudgeon you are still not defeated until you exhaust your follow-up attempts. **Can and will you do this?**

Enter Your Responses and Action Steps

Mehdi's Success Tool # 12

Fact finding is one of your most important functions. Without complete information you will not adequately understand the prospect's problems, or uncover the most effective solutions.

Proper fact finding is essential for your maximum success.

You must also have the proper tools (such as objective fact finder forms) and a procedure for how you continue to "bore in" to get all of the facts.

Where can you learn Advanced Fact Finding? *(see Recommended Sources)*

Enter Your Responses and Action Steps

Mehdi's Success Tool # 13

Remember who you are, and remember that you are always you.

People who "see you" should not see different and varied versions of you.

Even when you are not aware of it, other persons are constantly viewing you, and some are appraising whether or not they would or could do business with you.

Always look sharp when you are "seen" and always be mentally sharp (alert) when you are "on display".

What does the above mean to you?

Enter Your Responses and Action Steps

Mehdi's Success Tool # 14

Selling has been described as a "hurt" and "rescue" activity.

This can be stated another way: Selling is a "problem" and "solution" activity.

Can you find out what this means in the way you do business, and practice this?

Identify the "hurt" or "problem" and then present your "rescue" or "solution."

Enter Your Responses and Action Steps

Mehdi's Success Tool # 15

Understand that your prospect will only become your client and purchase or invest through you because he or she **wants to do so**.

Your clients must desire to deal with you. You must help make this possible for them. This means you must be a person of high class, integrity, honor, and intelligence – a person that they can be truly comfortable with.

Your prospects often need encouragement to take appropriate action. Always be encouraging to your prospects.

Can you figure-out realistic and practical ways to help your prospect understand and accept how to take the desired action now?

Enter Your Responses and Action Steps

Mehdi's Success Tool # 16

Selling, as the cliché goes, means selling yourself first. You can best do this in a low-key and natural manner, not by being over-attentive, highly ingratiating, super friendly, loud, talkative, funny, or totally compliant. You do not have to be the most agreeable person on earth to sell. People who strive to be extremely agreeable often burn-out quickly.

Financial sales professionals who do 'anything and everything' to please, while endlessly giving of their emotions, often become emotionally drained or spent. If you can learn to really care about the welfare of others, and allow this to show or be realized, then you can sell.

Will you learn to care and allow your concern to be obvious in sincere ways?

Enter Your Responses and Action Steps

Mehdi's Success Tool # 17

Once you master effective selling, or after you learn how to sell, realize that folks often buy from you because they want to, not because they need to. You have become a person they **like and trust**.

I often have people wanting to buy from me when they do not need to do so. You and I have the duty and responsibility to know our client's circumstances well and never sell them something they do not need or something that is not the best product for them, just because it is easy to make such sales. Never sell anything just because you can.

Will you have the courage to do this - and tell your client the truth?

Enter Your Responses and Action Steps

Mehdi's Success Tool # 18

An effective way to close a sale is with the alternate close.

Hopefully, you have already learned what an alternate close is.

Can you identify and practice the use of the alternate close?

In any good sales training course, the instructor should discuss these elements of basic selling, including the trial close.

If you have never heard these phrases, and do not know exactly how to employ the techniques, then you will profit from a basic sales training course.

Enter Your Responses and Action Steps

Mehdi's Success Tool # 19

You cannot become a successful financial planner without completing and passing the appropriate financial planning training courses. You must also learn how to operate, and regularly use, the appropriate financial planning software that covers the three essential areas:

- A **Client Relationship Management** (CRM) program such as *Practice Builder*.

- A **Comprehensive Planning** program, such as *Plan Builder*.

- A **Client Presentation** system, such as *Client Builder*. This strengthens your initial presentation.

If you are not highly pleased with your practice in these three vital areas, you should closely investigate these programs, designed by America's most experienced and successful financial advisors. *(see Recommended Sources)*

Enter Your Responses and Action Steps

Mehdi's Success Tool # 20

Yes, your prospect is expressing interest if he or she asks you the price of the service or product you are proposing. (This is referred to as a "buying" sign, and this is a valuable step in your selling process. Do not look on this as an objection.)

But any and every price is too high until you **justify with the benefits** for your prospect. Nothing can kill your sale like exposing the price **before** you detail the benefits.

Can you learn how to justify the price by explaining and personalizing the benefits?

Do you know what to do next?

Enter Your Responses and Action Steps

Mehdi's Success Tool # 21

Sometimes you meet people to sell and the paradigm is just not right for selling.

- So you must change the paradigm.
- What is a paradigm?
- What would be a good and bad paradigm...?

In order to reach a successful conclusion, you must change negative circumstances into positive circumstances.

How do you change your paradigm?

Enter Your Responses and Action Steps

Mehdi's Success Tool # 22

Successful selling is always based on **wants** more than **needs**. For a person who does not know there really is a need, there can be no wants.

It is easier for you to build on an existing desire than to create a new or different desire.

Can you elaborate on this, as this applies to your services and products?

Enter Your Responses and Action Steps

Mehdi's Success Tool # 23

Everyone needs approval with the believable stroking of their self-image.

How does this truth apply to you?

How can you accomplish this?

Enter Your Responses and Action Steps

Mehdi's Success Tool # 24

When your prospect objects to the **price** this often means that your prospect's **want** is not strong enough.

What can you do about this?

Would reducing the price solve this dilemma? In most areas of financial services it is not possible to reduce the price. **Therefore, what is the type of action that can help you reach a successful conclusion - that will solve your prospect's problem?**

Enter Your Responses and Action Steps

Mehdi's Success Tool # 25

Objections and denials that you receive from your prospect during a sales presentation are usually presented by them as a logical statement.

But most likely they are really emotional!

What should you do when you experience this?

Enter Your Responses and Action Steps

Mehdi's Success Tool # 26

Small doubts can often be resolved by answers to your questions.

Major doubts represent objections.

Objections require clarifying explanations.

Do you understand this process and can you more fully explain this truism?

Enter Your Responses and Personal Action Steps

Mehdi's Success Tool # 27

Skillful presentations of appropriate logic and reason can create the **reasonable urgency** and the **justification** for your prospect to make a positive decision …

…and most importantly, act now!

What are appropriate logic and reason, and how do you skillfully use or present these elements?

Enter Your Responses and Personal Action Steps

Mehdi's Success Tool # 28

If your prospects do not like you then they are not likely to buy from you.

- This is reasonable and universal.

- This dynamic occurs in China, the United States, Russia, Egypt; or any place on earth.

- What are sufficient reasons to cause your clients to keep liking you?

How do you keep your prospect(s) liking you?

Enter Your Responses and Personal Action Steps

Mehdi's Success Tool # 29

Talk with all of your prospects (as well as with your clients) foremost about their interests, not about your own.

However, you can make your interests relate to their interests.

How can you accomplish the above?

Enter Your Responses and Personal Action Steps

Mehdi's Success Tool # 30

Never feel that you know in advance what your client needs most until you have done **proper fact finding.** This always includes:

- Their family circumstances

- Their employment or career status

- Accurate and complete financial information

- All of the relevant emotional data.

How will you accomplish this?

Enter Your Responses and Personal Action Steps

Mehdi's Success Tool # 31

Control the **dynamics** of every interview as much as possible.

Suppose you call on a prospect who is a coin collector and this prospect mostly wants to show and explain his coin collection to you. It could be photos, furniture, their car, or any items of which they are proud or pleased.

How can you reasonably control the prevailing dynamics so that you are more likely to accomplish your mission?

Enter Your Responses and Personal Action Steps

Mehdi's Success Tool # 32

Realize that you are an intrusion on your prospect - until you become an interesting and appealing encounter.

How do you quickly become an interesting and appealing encounter?

What techniques could you adopt and apply to achieve this?

Enter Your Responses and Personal Action Steps

Mehdi's Success Tool # 33

You should always stay focused on your mission.

Explain this please?

Do you have a written Mission Statement? Your Mission Statement is not simply "to make more money" or "have a good life." Nearly every person who has achieved greatness has had a powerful and compelling sense of mission. The odds of your success will increase if you develop a clear mission statement – and repeat your mission statement often to yourself and to others. You should incorporate your mission statement into your marketing message and description of your services.

Write notes for your mission statement below, and refine your mission statement as often as necessary.

Enter Notes Here For Your Mission Statement

Mehdi's Success Tool # 34

It has been said by many sales coaches and trainers,

> *If you create enough interest and appeal no prospect will be too busy to consider your proposal.*

Is this a realistic goal for you?

What practices, skills, or knowledge will help you to achieve this?

Can you start action on this now?

Enter Your Responses and Personal Action Steps

Mehdi's Success Tool # 35

You can capture attention in many inappropriate ways. Some attention capturing ways that are not appropriate include screaming, talking too loud, "jerking" your prospect around, excessive physical contact, teasing, and even throwing papers at your prospect.

What other attention capturing techniques used by salespersons have you observed that are clearly not appropriate? No doubt you have even heard other "bad habits" recommended to you from so-called sales gurus.

How can you conduct yourself so as to never have anyone feel that you have "crossed the line" into negative or offensive behavior?

Enter Your Responses and Personal Action Steps

Mehdi's Success Tool # 36

Some excellent and appropriate "attention grabbers" that you might use include the following:

- Solutions
- Curiosity
- Fears of not being protected
- Pride

What are some additional appropriate ways you can ethically capture the attention of your prospects?

Enter Other Appropriate Ways and Your Action Steps

Mehdi's Success Tool # 37

You can usually arouse your prospect by offering:

- A better solution
- A more affordable solution
- More spendable income now
- More spendable income later

How can the above points help you?

Enter Responses and Action Steps

Mehdi's Success Tool # 38

You must always make clear the reasons - or ways - in which your recommended offering is affordable.

Remember, these reasons, or ways, must be clearly perceived by your prospect. It is not sufficient that you believe your recommendation is affordable; affordability must be absolutely recognized by the prospect before any purchase will be made. This is true, whether you present services, such as a comprehensive plan, portfolio management, or a specific product.

Why is this necessary?

What techniques could you adopt that would assure your prospect has reached your conclusion?

Enter Your Responses and Personal Action Steps

Mehdi's Success Tool # 39

It is most difficult to sell to a person who cannot think or reason well!

This can also apply to a person who is not paying attention. What might be the reasons an intelligent prospect is not paying attention to you?

Thus, in such a case, what should you do?

Hint: You should help the prospect follow your thinking or follow your reasoning.

How do you accomplish this?

Enter Your Responses and Personal Action Steps

Mehdi's Success Tool # 40

You must ask your prospect **questions** that enable and encourage your prospect to first bring up the solution you are about to propose to their specific need.

Can you create some examples of questions that might achieve this objective?

Enter Your Examples Here

Mehdi's Success Tool # 41

Accurately describing your prospect's problem, without any inappropriate embellishing, will help focus your prospect mentally.

This action will also help convince your prospects of their legitimate need.

How can you do this?

Enter Your Responses and Personal Action Steps

Mehdi's Success Tool # 42

Just as you methodically and consistently make sales, you can methodically and consistently generate qualified referrals. **How?**

Hint: There are a number of ways. Here is one: Nourish long-term relationships with other influential advisors. That means anyone who gives advice to others. These are your A-list clients, accountants, attorneys (especially tax and estate specialists), physicians, judges, planned giving advisors, bank trust officers, government officials, consultants, salespeople, and others.

You can target specific advisors with special efforts.

Enter How You Can Generate Referrals from Advisors

Mehdi's Success Tool # 43

Regularly attend select local, regional, and national related association and industry meetings and conventions - then network with other meeting participants, as well as with the featured presenters.

Interact to learn, and to get ideas. Interact to build working liaisons with others.

What are the benefits to you from doing this?

How can you improve in this aspect of your career?

Enter Your Responses and Personal Action Steps

Mehdi's Success Tool # 44

You may not believe this but I get referrals from other financial professionals that you might consider to be my competitors!

From time-to-time they prefer to not engage in certain business or approach certain people. These other financial professionals know they can trust me to **do what is right** and be supportive of them, and not take any other sales away from them. They also know I will act only to serve the client's best interest.

Why and how should you cultivate other financial professionals?

Enter Your Responses and Personal Action Steps

Mehdi's Success Tool # 45

Ask your A-list clients, when you are reviewing with them, or at any appropriate face to face gathering, who their other advisors are and who will they recommend?

Obviously these other advisors can become clients for you, or they can interface with you to serve mutual clients. Gradually they can become a source of high-quality referrals.

Can you do this?

Enter Your Responses and Personal Action Steps

Mehdi's Success Tool # 46

A conversation means the other person gets to talk also. Too many sales persons attempt to dominate all conversations.

When both people can speak easily and openly what does this accomplish?

Answer: Less tension and more effective communication.

How do you make certain that your prospect speaks enough?

Enter Your Responses and Personal Action Steps

Mehdi's Success Tool # 47

Presenting the correct answers (without undue embellishment) will satisfy your prospect's ego and need to dominate.

Why is this important for you?

How can you strengthen your use of this concept?

Enter Your Responses and Personal Action Steps

Mehdi's Success Tool # 48

You must trigger your prospect's **buying decision**.

How do you discover the critical element that will trigger your prospect's buying decision?

Note: If you don't know the critical element, and you need to employ it in the close, then simply ask. You might say, "What is the most important item I can help you accomplish?

What other technique or question might uncover this item?

Enter Your Responses and Personal Action Steps

Mehdi's Success Tool # 49

Each question from you turns your presentation into an interview.

Your prospects prefer to be interviewed, as opposed to feeling that they are being dominated. However, it takes skill and concentration to run an interview in a mutually rewarding fashion.

How do you transform your presentation into an interview?

Enter Your Responses and Personal Action Steps

Mehdi's Success Tool # 50

Often you must disturb your prospect's existing mental conclusion or disrupt their comfort zone.

Why is this often necessary?

What are the typical "existing conditions" of your prospects that must be disturbed?

What techniques or questions could you use to achieve this?

Enter Your Responses and Personal Action Steps

Mehdi's Success Tool # 51

Why are your questions so important?

Answer: Because your questions force your prospect to focus, think, and reply.

Also, your questions are how you gain information, and your questions enable you to reach mutual understanding.

Can you formulate and arrange questions in an order that will move you in your desired direction?

Enter Your Responses and Personal Action Steps

Mehdi's Success Tool # 52

Most people do not like long presentations or speeches.

Why should you avoid lengthy presentations or speeches?

Answer: Because you want to sell to the people you are speaking with, not annoy your prospect.

Can you elaborate on this?

Enter Your Responses and Personal Action Steps

Mehdi's Success Tool # 53

Yes, it is true, and rightly so - your prospect is thinking:

What's in it for me?

What does this fact tell you to do?

Enter Your Responses and Personal Action Steps

Mehdi's Success Tool # 54

As in show business, **always leave them wanting more** of you.

This means stop being charming, wonderful, pleasant, interesting, amusing, and marvelous (talking, socializing, interacting, etc.) and go away.

Do not stay until your prospect or audience is silently praying that you will stop and depart.

Why are most people, especially those who are speaking, selling, preaching, teaching, or instructing often unable to conclude and leave while they are still well received?

Enter Your Responses and Personal Action Steps

Mehdi's Success Tool # 55

Your facts and benefits must be believable!

How do you assure that your facts and benefits are believable?

Have you ever felt that you missed a sale because of a lack of credibility? If so, and it is likely to have happened, what might you do in the future to prevent this impression?

Can you prompt yourself to do this in every interview?

Enter Your Responses and Personal Action Steps

Mehdi's Success Tool # 56

Objections and turn-downs are not always permanent. Many of my greatest sales are reached after several attempts have been made to arrive at a purchase decision.

This also applies to your attempts to gain an appointment to meet with a top prospect. You know the modified phrase, "If at first you don't succeed, then try, try, try, and try until you succeed!"

Therefore, what follow-up action (or conduct) should be attempted by you?

Enter Your Responses and Personal Action Steps

Mehdi's Success Tool # 57

Intangibles, such as insurance, investments, or comprehensive advice are more challenging to illustrate or demonstrate.

Intangibles are often more difficult to place values on than others.

Thus, intangibles are more difficult to sell – and that is one reason why those selling intangibles generally earn a lot more than those selling clothing, appliances, vehicles or other tangibles.

How can you compensate for this?

Enter Your Responses and Personal Action Steps

Mehdi's Success Tool # 58

Your sales only go where they are invited and appreciated.

Your message will only be appreciated when someone feels that you really care about them – personally.

This fact dictates "what" regarding your conduct?

Enter Your Responses and Personal Action Steps

Mehdi's Success Tool # 59

Emotional decisions are usually fast coming - and final.

How can you encourage this?

Obviously the emotional decision must be positive for you to successfully conclude the proposed transaction.

How can you strengthen the likelihood of a positive appraisal?

Logical decisions are usually slow in coming.

Logical decisions may also be subject to revision.

Is there anything that you can do to help improve this?

Enter Your Responses and Personal Action Steps

Mehdi's Success Tool # 60

When your prospect stalls or delays, this is the time to use what we often refer to as *hurt and rescue* techniques.

Can you explain your techniques for executing this?

Enter Your Answers and Personal Action Steps

Mehdi's Success Tool # 61

It can be a long way from being "sold" to "purchasing now."

Can you explain the difference?

How can you employ this principle in your sales presentations?

Enter Your Responses and Personal Action Steps

Mehdi's Success Tool # 62

Visualizing is emotional circumstance.

Visualizing can be a powerful force, for or against you, in any selling situation.

What does "visualizing" mean?

How can you use this to your sales advantage?

Enter Your Responses and Personal Action Steps

Mehdi's Success Tool # 63

Confirming with facts or reason is logic.

What does this sentence mean to you?

Which is more powerful, logic or emotion?

How can you use this to your sales advantage?

Enter Your Responses and Personal Action Steps

Mehdi's Success Tool # 64

Never again will your prospect be this interested.

How can you make the most of this fact?

If you cannot gain sufficient interest now for a positive decision, how can you exit gracefully and then return with additional "ammunition" to close the sale?

Enter Your Responses and Personal Action Steps

Mehdi's Success Tool # 65

As a salesperson you must always nourish your relationships with both your clients and prospects.

How can you be nourishing?

Many large corporations are now employing the principles of Client Relationship Management (**CRM**) to achieve this. Have you considered how to apply this to your practice? Are you nurturing your clients in an efficient manner, to retain their business and receive an ongoing flow of referrals? (see Recommended Sources)

Enter Your Responses and Personal Action Steps

Mehdi's Success Tool # 66

Do you think selling is beneath you?

Is selling a low-class profession?

Don't successful doctors, lawyers, and professors also sell?

Can you debunk these misconceptions?

Can you "know" the truth about sales abilities and feel good about selling?

Why is understanding ethical selling beneficial for you?

Enter Your Responses and Personal Action Steps

Mehdi's Success Tool # 67

Testimonials can be reassuring for your prospects.

How can you get and use testimonials?

What are some creative ways to announce, reveal or display your testimonials?

Enter Your Responses and Personal Action Steps

Mehdi's Success Tool # 68

Every contact with a prospect should always contribute to the prospect's confidence in you and your recommendations.

How can you benefit from knowing this?

What about the contacts made by you through automation, or for you by a member of your staff? While not as significant as contact by you, wouldn't these help maintain the confidence of your prospect or client?

Are you familiar with how to use "drip marketing" to automate this?

Enter Your Responses and Personal Action Steps

Mehdi's Success Tool # 69

Close the sale, close your mouth, and close the door.

I just repeated – in different words this time – something that I have pointed out to you before.

What am I saying here?

Enter Your Responses and Personal Action Steps

Mehdi's Success Tool # 70

People buy **benefits** – as opposed to making a positive purchase decision based on well-answered **objections**.

Please explain this?

Isn't this similar to the comment that people buy personal benefits, not product features?

Don't many weak sales persons depend on features, rather than focusing on the benefits?

Enter Your Responses and Personal Action Steps

Mehdi's Success Tool # 71

On some occasions you may need to convince your prospect that his or her problem or situation is worse than they realize.

This is not an easy task. This is also not a task that you are looking forward to, but this must be done, just as the physician often has to tell patients that they have a serious health issue.

How can you accomplish this difficult task without deception?

Enter Your Responses and Personal Action Steps

Mehdi's Success Tool # 72

Your "enemies" are hesitations, objections, stalls, refusals, and rejections. Your biggest enemy is ignorance.

Why is it important to know your enemies and how to combat or defeat them?

What additional "enemies" do financial services salespersons often encounter?

What can you do to prevent your enemies from winning over you?

Enter Your Responses and Personal Action Steps

Mehdi's Success Tool # 73

This old truism still stands firmly.

Do not suppress objections. Identify objections and conquer them!

How can you achieve this?

Enter Your Responses and Personal Action Steps

Mehdi's Success Tool # 74

Why is it better to prevent an objection than to answer an objection?

List the three top objections that you have encountered most often in your career. Then with each one, list the steps you might take that would have an impact on preventing that objection from ever being raised by your prospect.

Is there any reason why you can't employ prevention?

Enter Your Responses and Personal Action Steps

Mehdi's Success Tool # 75

A stall at closing could result from many different sources. The three most common reasons you will encounter are:

  1. Lack of realized ability to purchase.

  2. Lack of sufficient want.

  3. Not fully understanding the importance of the problem and the solution.

How can you prevent stalls that result from these causes?

Enter Your Responses and Personal Action Steps

Mehdi's Success Tool # 76

A want, or wants, must be aroused.

How can you arouse wants?

Based on the nature of the products or services that you offer, what are the most powerful wants that you can explain?

How can you get the prospect to articulate these wants, and emphasize them as you attempt to close the sale?

Enter Your Responses and Personal Action Steps

Mehdi's Success Tool # 77

You are always dealing with your prospect's self-image.

How can you protect and/or "play to" your prospect's self-image?

Is it possible that you have sometimes allowed your image to overpower that of your prospect? Generally this will kill the opportunity to close a sale, or maintain a client. Remember, your goal is to make the sale, not to achieve some military victory. You want a positive image, not a powerful, controlling image.

Are you making regular efforts to improve your image in your market area and in your profession? Have you considered hiring an image builder?

Enter Your Responses and Personal Action Steps

Mehdi's Success Tool # 78

Only a few elements or actions are vital and absolutely essential.

One of your key and most important elements is the image you create, establish, and maintain in your market place.

What image-building steps by other professionals in your community have been particularly successful?

What specific efforts have you taken to create, establish, and maintain your image as being unique, special, precious, and highly-qualified in your market area? Are you positioned as the market leader?

Enter Your Responses and Personal Action Steps

Mehdi's Success Tool # 79

Be out there. See the people. Interact. Be actively engaged. Stay involved. Meet people.

My late dear friend, the great insurance sales agent **Ben Feldman**, once gave a sales talk to a large audience and he said only one three-word sentence and then departed the stage.

He said, "See the people!"

Yes you must see the people. Today the people must also see you. Today people must know you, warm to you, relate to you. Do what gets you noticed and accepted.

- Good things happen most when your time is busy with productive experiences.

- Your productive habits mean productive time.

When you are not 'out there' among your prospect types, find time to 'get noticed' in other ways. **What are some other appropriate ways?** Here are some answers:

- Write an article.

- Be a person quoted in another person's article.

- Send copies of these articles to your clients, prospects, and other professionals, including your local media.

- Obtain a speaking opportunity.

- Form and chair a committee to research something.

- Be photographed with a popular local leader.

- Send a news release with a photo and info on an appropriate topic.

- Give a motivational talk to a children's athletic league. Be a team sponsor. Be photographed with them.

- Arrange photos of yourself in the act of doing a good deed, or making any 'good citizen' effort, then exploit the publicity value.

- Sponsor a contest for students – at any level.

There are countless other ways for you to be *favorably noticed.*

Create and execute a list of what might work for you.

Enter Your Responses and Personal Action Steps

Mehdi's Success Tool # 80

Your image will take care of itself. **FALSE!**

If your image takes care of itself it will present you as just another financial services salesperson, or a typical salesperson trying to push a product. Your products and services will be perceived as merely "ordinary" if you make no efforts to enhance your image.

Many financial services sales reps ignore their image and reputation, in the false belief that their responsible behavior will establish a widely recognized and accepted reputation for them. Unfortunately this does not happen – they remain largely unknown and unappreciated.

To exhibit what is unique, special, and precious about you requires specific and special building image efforts.

What should you do about creating your image? What steps should you consider to actually gain and maintain recognition and greater status in your market area?

Enter Your Responses and Personal Action Steps

Mehdi's Success Tool # 81

If you are waiting to be discovered by your prospects then you are very unlikely to ever be noticed or recognized. You must cause the recognition to result. Consider your options to build your reputation (or image) over time:

- Can you promote yourself skillfully? Is self-promotion the most effective use of your time?

- Should you consider using a media advocate?

- Can you afford a full services financial PR firm?

Remember: *You will seldom get any positive publicity by accident.*

Enter Your Responses and Personal Action Steps

Mehdi's Success Tool # 82

If you do not position yourself in your market then your competition will position you - to their advantage, not to your advantage. Consider the following issues:

- **What is your market area?**

- **Which demographic groups do you serve?**

- **How can your target prospects be reached effectively?**

- **How do you position yourself as the market leader where you are?**

Enter Your Responses and Personal Action Steps

Mehdi's Success Tool # 83

The tougher your prospect, the more you should …?

Answer: Reassure by stroking the self-image of your prospect.

How can you do this without being devious?

Enter Your Responses and Personal Action Steps

Mehdi's Success Tool # 84

You must modify or adjust your entire encounter, conduct and words, according to your prospect's personality.

How is this possible for you?

Answer: There is not one specific correct answer for everyone. But when you are not sure what to do you can usually depend on your common sense.

Enter Your Common Sense Response

Mehdi's Success Tool # 85

You must program my tools (that you select) plus your additional techniques into your habitual practices, but not become a robot.

You must also allow yourself sufficient freedom and flexibility to operate effectively as yourself. Remember, you are unique.

How will you do this?

Enter Your Responses and Personal Action Steps

Mehdi's Success Tool # 86

At the beginning of your encounter (by phone, mail, e-mail, face to face, or whatever) you must promise your prospect an easy exit from the meeting with you, plus an early benefit for meeting with you. Once in a meeting you cannot hold your prospect captive. Your prospect must feel free to terminate the meeting at any moment.

Can you recall incidents where you have failed to do this?

Successful positioning at the earlier stages is largely avoidance of making the traditional mistakes.

Can you describe examples of how you can impress on your prospect early benefits for a modest investment of his or her time?

Enter Your Responses and Your Action Steps

Mehdi's Success Tool # 87

As quickly as possible, you must convince your prospects that they have a need, problem, or a situation, that should be (must be) resolved in their best interest as soon as possible.

Describe how you can do this?

Enter Your Responses and Personal Action Steps

Mehdi's Success Tool # 88

Your prospect's degree of warmth toward you influences how you modify or adjust your approach and conduct your encounter.

What does this mean to you?

Please describe an example of this?

Enter Your Example(s)

Mehdi's Success Tool # 89

Your prospect's degree of intelligence influences how you modify or adjust your approach and complete your initial encounter.

What does this mean?

Please describe an example of this?

Enter Your Example(s)

Mehdi's Success Tool # 90

You are what your habits cause to take place. You will receive the results of your habits. You will have what your habits have caused to result.

Your habits are what you do repeatedly, whether by intent or neglect.

What do you often do to make sales?

Are there some habits you should seek to adopt more regularly?

Isn't it possible that adding additional positive habits would have a major impact on your success? Can you list the beneficial habits you would like to increase?

Enter Your Responses and Your Action Steps

Mehdi's Success Tool # 91

It is okay to be bold, if you are confident, sure, and in command.

Why is this so?

At what point in your initial interviews would this be the most effective?

Enter Your Responses and Personal Action Steps

Mehdi's Success Tool # 92

A good phone attitude, or a good phone personality, is essential for your phone sales success. A poor phone attitude, or poor "phone personality," can kill your sales.

Do you know how to always use the phone to your sales benefit?

Hint: You have no doubt read of the concept of placing a mirror in front of yourself when making phone calls. **Have you wondered why this simple move is so effective?** You are not likely to frown or scowl at yourself while watching your reflection. As you make calls you will smile, even laugh, at yourself. This will improve your voice and help you sound more appealing.

Enter Your Responses and Action Steps

Mehdi's Success Tool # 93

Always be in command of your specialty. Do not fake anything.

If your prospect mentions (or makes-up) the title of a book do not say that you have read that book.

Prospects may test you to see if you are securely in command, and if you will tell the truth, or attempt to bluff them into believing you are widely read or known.

Why is it important for you to be "in secure command" of your specialty?

Enter Your Conclusions

Mehdi's Success Tool # 94

Your pre-approach, follow-up, and individual prospect planning demand as much care and attention to details, as your actual sales encounter.

How do you arrange for, and execute, your pre-approach, follow-up, and related planning?

How could you improve your performance in these areas?

Indicate Your Responses and Personal Action Steps

Mehdi's Success Tool # 95

As soon as possible find the decision maker.

Always talk to the decision maker.

An estimated two-thirds of the lost sales take place because the person to whom you are speaking does not have the authority (family or business control) to make the purchase decision.

Explain how you can identify and locate the decision make?

Enter Your Responses and Personal Action Steps

Mehdi's Success Tool # 96

A pre-written script, cards with key notes, or a PowerPoint display with important reminders of key highlights, can be very helpful for almost any occasion you experience.

Do you make it a regular practice to use a written agenda for all client meetings? Can you imagine a corporate board of directors planning a meeting with no agenda?

Do you understand why this is so?

Please elaborate?

Enter Your Responses and Action Steps

Mehdi's Success Tool # 97

Mortgage insurance sales represent an ongoing need among most of your prospects.

Realize that the owners of closely held companies or professional practices normally sign personally on all corporate notes, and that these loans are callable upon death. **Do you always ask such clients about their business notes?**

How can you quickly master the proven fundamentals of mortgage insurance sales?

Enter Your Thoughts and Self-Action Steps

Mehdi's Success Tool # 98

Your prospect may also test you with an attempt to uncover the best deal.

Their "test" often involves money amounts or payment methods.

Sometimes they will ask for a discount, rebate, kick-back, or bribe.

Can you handle this effectively?

Enter Your Responses and Related Action Steps

Mehdi's Success Tool # 99

Sincere enthusiasm is a valuable asset for financial sales.

Product knowledge is equally important to enthusiasm or to any of your other sales factors.

However, enthusiasm works against you if it is obviously faked.

How can you maintain sincere enthusiasm?

Enter Your Responses and Planned Action Steps

Mehdi's Success Tool # 100

Always suppress your enthusiasm until you have appropriate reasons to display your enthusiasm.

Otherwise you may appear to be insincere, pretending, or even idiotic.

How can you know when to display your enthusiasm?

Enter Your Remarks and Personal Action Steps

Mehdi's Success Tool # 101

You have specific advantages over your competition.

What are your specific advantages?

It is important for you to list those advantages you have now – and also those you can easily increase and legitimately exploit in your march toward sales supremacy. Please list your advantages now….

Enter Your Responses and Personal Action Steps

Mehdi's Success Tool # 102

Yes, the old cliché is still true:

> *Most prospects do not care what you know –*
> *until they know that you care about them.*

What does this truism mean you should always do?

Enter Your Responses and Personal Action Steps

Mehdi's Success Tool # 103

Your most beneficial sales assets are your success habits.

Habits are not habits unless you use them continually, repeat them often, and apply them over and over again.

Your success habits may include use of your product knowledge, maintaining your desired image within your market area, use of your financial software, ways that you maintain your motivation, etc.

What success habits can you add to this list?

Enter Additional Success Habits You Can Acquire

Mehdi's Success Tool # 104

One of your most essential, most helpful, and most beneficial, sales and success assets is knowing how to get maximum use from your computer, software, and the internet.

Are you sufficiently computer literate?

    Can you use the word processor to prepare attractive proposals?
    Can you use Excel to analyze or display financial relationships?
    Can you use presentation software effectively?
    Are you using social media to communicate informally?
    Are you comfortable using Google and Wikipedia for research?
    Have you investigated www.PlaniPedia.org?

Do you have the correct software and a proper web site, plus other internet advantages – all working for you?

Indicate Your Reaction and Personal Action Steps

Mehdi's Success Tool # 105

Today's thinking is what you will believe tomorrow.

What most influences your current and ongoing thinking about sales?

Do you regularly read books about business or economic trends? Do you read trade magazines? Attend workshops or conventions? Study sales literature from any source?

Do you use a "Reading Service" to provide you with an abbreviated summary or digest of the most significant thought-shaping volumes?

Enter Your Responses and Personal Action Steps

Mehdi's Success Tool # 106

You were born with everything you need to win. You can win big-time!

Do you understand why this is an accurate statement?

Enter Your Responses and Personal Action Steps

Mehdi's Success Tool # 107

Most of your sales problems originate in your own mind.

This is where most of your sales failures begin. The old cliché is true: You are your own worst enemy.

In your own mind is also where most of your sales problems and sales failures can be solved.

Explain this?

Enter Your Responses and Personal Action Steps

Mehdi's Success Tool # 108

Be your own First Sergeant.

Give yourself pep-talks, self-instructions, self-critiques – and if necessary, even scoldings. You deserve help from a source that truly has your best interest at heart.

What are "self pushes" and self pep-talks?

Enter Your Responses and Personal Action Steps

Mehdi's Success Tool # 109

There is no logical reason why you should "go-it-alone" when there are many sources of valuable information that you should and could be regularly tapping.

What is a valuable free source of weekly sales and marketing information that is actually useful and often motivational?

Enter Your Responses and Personal Action Steps

Mehdi's Success Tool # 110

Believe that you are successful and that you are going to become even more successful – and that you will achieve greater success sooner, rather than later.

Set specific time limits for your realistic goals. Create a track to follow to reach your goals.

Figure-out how to accomplish this – Start Now!

Enter Your Responses and Personal Action Steps

Mehdi's Success Tool # 111

Yes, your attitude is (almost) everything!

And your positive attitude should be consistent or habitual.

How can you make a habit of having a beneficial attitude?

Self motivation is a habit of your thoughts.

Explain this?

What steps can you take on a regular basis to motivate yourself? Would you benefit from increased effort in this area? **What would be some outstanding sources to help you accelerate your improvement?**

Enter Your Responses and Personal Action Steps

Mehdi's Success Tool # 112

Attempting "anything" or "whatever" leads to failure in your financial sales career. Your sales efforts must be planned and carefully focused.

You must focus on, and always use only the **specific** procedures that you select as the procedures that work best for you.

Please explain this in detail?

Enter Your Explanation and Action Steps

Mehdi's Success Tool # 113

You must always have some flexibility.

Tires may suddenly go flat or gradually leak air. Things change. Life means growth and growth means change.

People get sick or arrive late due to traffic problems.

Why is flexibility important for you to function most effectively?

Why is flexibility also important for you to understand and accept in others?

Enter Your Responses and Personal Action Steps

Mehdi's Success Tool # 114

Super sales achievers are super planners first.

Can you effectively "plan" your financial sales efforts?

Enter Your Responses and Personal Action Steps

Mehdi's Success Tool # 115

A simple rule for getting the most from your time is to always be aware of whether what you are doing is directly contributing to the results you desire.

Your time is spent either being productive or not being productive.

You choose how your time is invested. Be honest about how you classify your time and efforts.

Why is your time especially important for you?

Enter Your Responses and Personal Action Steps

Mehdi's Success Tool # 116

No, goal setting is not obsolete! Most truisms stand forever

Goal setting is usually doable, practical, and helpful.

But your goals are only dreams, or mere fantasies, unless you have:

    A. Practical "proper action plans" that…
    B. Contain a realistic action course, over a…
    C. Specific time period, one that …
    D. Includes your target deadlines.

How can you achieve realistic goals that you set?

Enter Your Responses and Action Steps

Mehdi's Success Tool # 117

You must continually adapt your selling effort to market changes.

What are market changes, in general?

What are the challenges and changes most likely to be experienced in your target market?

What steps could you be making to adapt better for the future?

Enter Your Responses and Personal Action Steps

Mehdi's Success Tool # 118

Few agents or planners have a well organized procedure for prospecting.

What is your prospecting procedure? Are you satisfied with your current prospecting results?

Do you have a written prospecting or client acquisition plan?

Enter Your Responses and Personal Action Steps

Mehdi's Success Tool # 119

Few agents or planners have a well organized procedure for marketing. Do you recognize the difference between prospecting (for individuals) and marketing (for maximum area penetration) in your target area?

What are your marketing procedures? Are you satisfied with your marketing results?

Do you have a written **Marketing Plan**? Is this incorporated into your overall **Business Plan**?

If your marketing/business plans exists already, do you review and revise them on a schedule that you established?

Enter Your Responses and Personal Action Steps

Mehdi's Success Tool # 120

Unfortunately it can take many years to learn how things work in real life!

How can you speed-up this process?

Should you make some modifications (improvements) here?

Enter Your Responses and Personal Action Steps

Mehdi's Success Tool # 121

Are you willing to invest in yourself – in your personal improvement – or not?

How can you prove your answer?

Which areas of self-improvement would pay the biggest dividends for you – short term and long term?

Have you ever created a one-page **Self-Improvement Plan**? Why not prepare one now, by jotting down the areas you feel need improvement.

Enter Your Responses and Personal Action Steps

Mehdi's Success Tool # 122

Your life, work, earnings, and career all advance the most when you stay focused on your **objectives,** rather than on your prior accomplishments.

Please explain why?

Enter Your Responses and Action Steps

Mehdi's Success Tool # 123

It is okay to fail. Failure does not have to be final for you.

Six people who *claimed* they did not reach their potential in life were Ben Franklin, Abraham Lincoln, Albert Einstein, Thomas Edison, Henry Ford, and General George S. Patton.

Set your goals very high! **Why should you do so?**

Hint: You have massive potential once you have created and applied the "just right for you" success system.

Enter Your Responses and Personal Action Steps

Mehdi's Success Tool # 124

Successful people habitually make the best use of their time.

Super achievers don't find time, they make time. They **find** opportunities or they **create** opportunities.

They also delegate effectively so that they can focus their energy and time more profitably.

How are you at making the most productive use of your time?

Enter Your Responses and Personal Action Steps

Mehdi's Success Tool # 125

Winning requires concessions.

Can you give up that which gradually harms your productivity?

Which bad habits are harming your productivity now? You have eliminated some bad habits in your past, and this can be accomplished again. **You could do this again, couldn't you?**

Write Your Responses and Personal Action Steps

Mehdi's Success Tool # 126

Laughter can make your work more enjoyable. Laughter helps you to lighten-up.

Laughter helps you to be much more flexible. **Where or how do you experience fun?**

You can increase your "fun and laughter" activities. Start by listing here the "fun and laughter" activities that you can increase.

Enter Your Responses and Personal Action Steps

Mehdi's Success Tool # 127

You (and you alone – or with the help of a coach) will decide if you win or if you fail to achieve your clear, realistic, and specific goals.

How will you determine this?

Enter Your Answer and the Steps You Will Take

Mehdi's Success Tool # 128

The right sales system for you will enable you to build your life and career on a solid foundation and ever-increasing success.

However, over time, you must revise your sales system to fit the changes in your market, and in your own capacity. Perhaps you should consider altering your system from time to time as you acquire additional selling techniques.

Will you complete each step in this success program and end-up with the tailored sales system that is most effective for you?

Enter Your Reply and Planned Actions

Mehdi's Success Tool # 129

You must always think for yourself.

Use your common sense above anything and everything that you are taught, told, instructed, cajoled, or conditioned into believing.

Can you acquire the habit of thinking, examining, and questioning?

Can you discontinue accepting everything at face value?

Enter Your Responses and Personal Action Steps

Mehdi's Success Tool # 130

Human life has, and always will, involve hardships, challenges, problems and unfairness.

Learn to grow the strength and courage you need to navigate each stage of your life and work, so you can win and be as happy as possible.

How can you achieve this?

Answer: By discovering, adopting, and habitually using the success system that works best for you.

Enter Your Thoughts and Personal Action Steps

Mehdi's Success Tool # 131

Love your prospects and clients - and you will do your very best to serve them. Love your clients and you will operate honestly in all ways and with lasting integrity. Love your clients and your clients will reciprocate by valuing you and loving to do business with you. Love your clients and you will genuinely care about them. Then it will be easy, even natural, for you to take ownership of their concerns and issues.

Can you love each one of them – warts and all?

Can you develop habits that will help you to "love" them?

Can you learn to be patient with, be understanding of, be tolerant with, and even be forgiving of, your clients and prospects?

Enter Your Responses and Personal Action Steps

Mehdi's Success Tool # 132

When you always approach and provide your prospects with love, fairness, and wisdom you create strong relationships.

Why are lasting relationships especially important for you?

Enter Your Answers and Personal Action Steps

Mehdi's Success Tool # 133

You maintain long-lasting relationships with your love, wisdom, outstanding service, attention to detail, constant contact, and by doing more than expected.

Can you do this month-after-month?

Enter How You Will Do This and Your Planned Methods

Mehdi's Success Tool # 134

Love enables your prospect to follow your lead better than the use of any other sales tool or strategy. This is a form of servant leadership

None of your clients or prospects receives enough love, attention, consideration, or respect.

Again I ask you...

Are you strong enough, and secure enough, to do this?

Enter Your Related Thoughts and Personal Action Steps

Mehdi's Success Tool # 135

Either you have sufficient discipline or you do not.

Your sales results boil down to this. Discipline means you get things done, and you get them done on time.

You make things happen! You do not wait. You do not even hesitate.

You have to do "detail work" like licking stamps or stuffing envelopes.

Can you find your discipline? Can you maintain sufficient discipline?

Enter Your Responses and Personal Action Steps

Mehdi's Success Tool # 136

You know that **referrals** are very important to your professional success. When your client or another professional gives you a name, this is a powerful endorsement. The referred person is pre-sold by their friend or associate having given you their name.

Don't assume you have received all the referrals!

Don't assume the referral is eager to do business with you!

You need to have a system for follow-up with the referral. Send a nice letter. Then send another letter and an article. Then maybe send some generic, non-product literature. The best prospects often are the hardest to reach, but will become the most valuable. Be gracious, but be persistent. Be sure to thank your referrer. Many successful advisors use a CRM program to automate this critical process.

If you don't have a referral system, will you acquire and use one?

Enter Your Responses and Personal Action Steps

Mehdi's Success Tool # 137

There are three main reasons why agents and planners fail. These are:

1. **Not carefully planning.**

2. **Not being disciplined but being lazy.**

3. **Not being strong enough to repeatedly do what must be done.**

Can you overcome these three factors?

Enter Your Responses and Personal Action Steps

Mehdi's Success Tool # 138

What comes about in your sales is what you do something about!

1. Your aggressive actions and interventions make the difference.

2. You are not a bystander.

3. You are not at the mercy of chance or luck.

It will be your efforts, not those of a manager, team leader, coach or a sales trainer that will determine your achievements.

Do you understand this? Will you act accordingly?

Enter Your Responses and Personal Action Steps

Mehdi's Success Tool # 139

Ask yourself: **What am I really doing to close the sales I seek?**

Are you making all the efforts you feel are appropriate? If not, which areas do you feel should be considered for your maximum efforts?

Enter Your Responses and Personal Action Steps

Mehdi's Success Tool # 140

When in doubt depend on your common sense!

Your common sense is far more likely to be correct in the long run than commentaries you hear in the media, or the preaching of the so-called self-help and sales gurus. After all, if they were so great, why would they not still be performing the actions they teach?

Will you remember to always use your common sense? Even when you are given ridiculous directives, like:

"Always push our Super HR Annuity plan"

"Promise anything to close the sale!"

"Say anything to make the sale, no one will remember!"

Enter Your Responses and Personal Action Steps

Mehdi's Success Tool # 141

When out of time, or when you are facing any trying situation, count on your common sense.

Sales are often lost when your common sense is not brought into play and acted upon!

Will you remain forever ready to use your common sense when needed?

Indicate Your Responses and Personal Action Steps

Mehdi's Success Tool # 142

Stress often comes from <u>not doing</u> what you know you <u>should do</u>.

Stress is not just a term regarding your mental attitude on one day. Stress can be a very destructive disease. Stress can rob you of your ability, energy, and much of your knowledge and good intentions. Learn which activities will help you to reduce personal stress.

Will you do what you know you should do regarding stress?

Enter Your Responses and Personal Action Steps

Mehdi's Success Tool # 143

We all have the same elements to deal with. I deal with all of these and you can also:

- The economy
- Endless taxes of all sorts
- Ever-changing regulations
- Difficult clients
- Stalling or evasive prospects
- Family problems
- Aging
- Personal illness
- Expenses
- People that do not do what they promise
- People that do not do what they are paid for doing
- Not enough talent or skill in various areas
- Not enough money to operate as preferred

Can you deal with these and still manage your habits to achieve peace of mind as well as sales success?

Enter Your Responses and Personal Action Steps

Mehdi's Success Tool # 144

Thomas Edison said, "There are no rules here. We are just trying to accomplish something."

For you I have rules that foster more productive habits. Acquiring additional proper habits results in higher sales for you! In this *Fast-Track* system I am sharing **everything** with you.

My rules became my habits. My habits became my tools. All of my tools are revealed here for you. These tools can make you number one in financial sales. But you must adopt the tools that work best for you and repeatedly apply those tools.

Will you stay with this program until you learn the system that is just right for you, and then practice your special system day in and day out?

Enter Your Responses and Personal Action Steps

Mehdi's Success Tool # 145

You must always deal with reality. Stay grounded.

Be careful (reluctant) about following so-called marketing gurus. Do not believe in your face offers like "Stop making the home office rich!" or "My secret system will make you an annuity millionaire in two months!" or "If you act now you can get my proven, never-fail $4,000 super-sales success secrets for just $25!"

Do not fall for claims of quick-and-easy outstanding results.

Are there any quick and easy ways to your outstanding sales success and professionalism?

Answer: No! No! No! But finding and using your "just right system" is faster than most routes to your greater success.

Enter Your Responses and Personal Action Steps

Mehdi's Success Tool # 146

Lots of good people are so busy surviving, doing what they are in the habit of doing, being self absorbed, or creating the soap opera of their lives that they just do not hear.

They try to listen. They look at you. But the words from another person do not register. They are busy thinking of what they can say next. They don't want you to talk. They may be too consumed by their own ideas.

Do you know how to penetrate and "get through to prospects?"

Can you cause your prospects to hear you?

Enter Your Responses and Personal Action Steps

Mehdi's Success Tool # 147

It is often impossible to listen while you are talking.

Listen to others.

When you talk, you must be understood.

But you must also listen carefully.

Can you truly accomplish both of these tasks?

Enter Your Responses and Personal Action Steps

Mehdi's Success Tool # 148

All of the additional money you are ever going to make is currently in the pockets of other people who are your prospects.

Can you serve them so that they will reach into their pockets?

Enter Your Responses and Personal Action Steps

Mehdi's Success Tool # 149

You must take responsibility for your circumstances and act accordingly.

How do you take responsibility and make your desired results happen?

Enter Your Responses and Personal Action Steps

Mehdi's Success Tool # 150

I often tell my students (who are agents, planners, or financial advisors) that Winston Churchill said, "If you are going through Hell, keep going."

Will you keep trying even during your most difficult times?

Hard times and difficult economic pressures make the simplest of solutions the most effective. This system of success tools has been continuously modified to help me serve my clients as they feel mounting financial pressure and economic concerns.

Will you apply these Tools now – for the benefit of your clients – and for yourself?

Enter Your Responses and Personal Action Steps

Mehdi's Success Tool # 151

If you don't have much going wrong then you don't have much going on.

Do you deal effectively with your problems that arise, as they arise?

Change is constant – for your clients and for you.

Will you continue to modify (as I have personally) **the application of these success tools, as necessary for your circumstances, when the economy worsens, and when it re-bounds?**

Enter Your Responses and Personal Action Steps

Mehdi's Success Tool # 152

The more you invest in your prospects and clients, the more you will accomplish for your prospects and clients and for yourself.

You can invest your time, your attention, and your interest.

These cost no cash – but can produce your greatest results!

Can you do this? Will you do this?

Enter Your Responses and Personal Action Steps

Mehdi's Success Tool # 153

Always do precisely what you say you are going to do.

When possible, do more than promised. Your promise made is your debt unpaid - until you fulfill your promise.

> Do things when you promise, be timely, or be early.

> Everyone notices.

Can you keep all of your promises to prospects and clients?

Do you make every effort to keep your promises?

Enter Your Responses and Personal Action Steps

Mehdi's Success Tool # 154

One major secret to your success is constancy of your purpose.

This gets us back to the dynamic that I used to begin this *Fast-Track* course: "Your habits will make you, or your habits will break you."

You are unique, special, and precious.

My earnest wish is that you develop and always practice the winning sales habits that produce the best results for you.

Will you? Are you now massing your resolve?

Enter Your Responses and Personal Action Steps

Mehdi's Success Tool # 155

Over time many agents and planners become inflexible in their routines.

They may feel they know everything that works for them.

They resist new methods and grow resentful of management's attempts to help. Many refuse to revise their methods – even when the economy plummets. They become locked into absolutes; they simply will not change. **Even the best of habits require modification!**

This is why "new people" will always come along and outsell all those "old people" who refused to change.

How can you avoid performing by rote and remain open to new ideas and methods?

Enter Your Responses and Personal Action Steps

Mehdi's Success Tool # 156

Why should you remain focused on the present?

Answer: This is where all your sales result.

Yes, it is good to have plans for future improvement, but your key is to be implementing new positive habits now. Ask yourself, what will I do this week, for sure, to improve my knowledge, skills and client acquisition?

Can you now list your improvement areas for this week?

Enter Your Improvement Areas and Personal Actions

Mehdi's Success Tool # 157

What does it take to cause your sales to soar?

Answer: Your largest amount of sales will be produced by following the sales system that works best for you. Your key is not luck or just hard work. Desired results will come from your proper action.

You can argue about your proper course of action - but why try to reinvent the wheel?

Enter Your Responses and Personal Action Steps

Mehdi's Success Tool # 158

Your prospect is not a target!

Your client is not someone to be exploited!

Your prospect or client is the person you want to partner with to create a win-win situation.

Can you be a worthy partner? Your client deserves the best!

Enter Your Responses and Personal Action Steps

Mehdi's Success Tool # 159

Your sales success results not from **what you know**. Your sales success results from how you **use what you know!**

Is this old adage still true? Explain?

Enter Your Explanation and Personal Action Steps

Mehdi's Success Tool # 160

What you are attempting (selling financial products and services) is meaningful. **It is a career with purpose and dignity**.

Your efforts will create an **extraordinary and positive impact** on the lives of your clients.

The selling aspect of your profession is not a humiliating experience that makes your specialty a second class career option.

Why are these facts important for you to accept?

Enter Your Responses and Personal Action Steps

Mehdi's Success Tool # 161

Your **Personal Mission Statement** explains and defines your purpose and goals.

Do you have a *Personal Mission Statement*?

Write your current condensed Mission Statement below.

Can you **improve** your brief *Personal Mission Statement*? Can you make it clearer, more precise, more inclusive, and if possible even briefer?

Enter Your Mission Statement and Action Steps

Mehdi's Success Tool # 162

The ***born salesman*** refers to a person with a ***good personality***.

But selling requires much more than a good personality. There are no born salesmen. The born salesman concept is a myth. Anyone can sell if he or she uses an effective sales system.

The right sales system for you enables you to do what it takes to get to the next sales level – until you close.

Will you stay with this program until you uncover the complete sales system that is just right for you?

What is your target date for when you will obtain this?

Enter Your Responses and Personal Action Steps

Mehdi's Success Tool # 163

You live and work in an era that is vastly more complex than in the former days of mostly door-to-door selling. Today all of your prospects are busy, visually oriented, media savvy, internet connected, better educated, more sophisticated, more jaded, more suspicious, more cynical and more exploited.

You must now earn your prospects' trust, inform and educate your prospects, address their concerns in an easy-to-understand way, and if possible, use an enjoyable or pleasant format.

All of this helps your prospects sell themselves. You should not "wing it" but stick to your proven sales system.

Can you master all of this?

Enter Your Responses and Personal Action Steps

Mehdi's Success Tool # 164

Pre-call planning means you prepare for a sale (or sales call) before meeting with your prospect.

Is this important for you?

How can you be better prepared?

- Do you have your papers organized in a folder?
- Do you always use a written agenda?
- Are you always ready at the assigned time for the interview?
- Do you follow a proven process (like the **IARFC** teaches)?

Should you be polishing your pre-call preparation skills?

Enter Your Responses and Personal Action Steps

Mehdi's Success Tool # 165

Always get your prospect's input before you present your sales offer.

Why is this important?

- **How can you plan to do this?**

- **What would you do or say?**

- **When should you present your specific recommendation?**

Enter Your Responses and Personal Action Steps

Mehdi's Success Tool # 166

Do not concentrate on your general goals.

Concentrate on the specific task you need to execute now that will move you toward your defined goals.

Why is this important?

What are the specific tasks you should address tomorrow?

- Please write down tomorrow's specific tasks – now!

- Now, for yourself, do them – for sure!

Enter Your Responses and Personal Action Steps

Mehdi's Success Tool # 167

Follow-up **immediately** after every sales call you complete or attempt.

Handwritten messages on professional looking note cards are especially effective. Write short messages, and then mail your note cards. This gives the impression that you are a professional, interested in the prospect, and that you take care of details. (Some advisors do these at home every evening.)

This habit also shows your thoughtfulness and promptness.

Can you hand write notes on appropriate business note cards?

Follow-up again and again, by various means, until your relationship is established. This prospect (or client) should be inserted into your **CRM** system – to assure regular communications and attention to future needs. (For details on **CRM** systems, see Recommended Sources.)

Enter Your Responses and Personal Action Steps

Mehdi's Success Tool # 168

Recognize and respect how your prospects and clients prefer to communicate with you.

- You must know their preference! You can ask about this.
- Do they prefer written letters, emails or phone calls?
- Do they like to receive copies of articles that might apply to them?

You must adjust your style to fit that of your prospect.

Can you become aware of your prospect's style of communication and respond accordingly?

Enter Your Responses and Personal Action Steps

Mehdi's Success Tool # 169

Plant triggers and leave footprints.

Triggers mean every time you interact with a client or prospect you provide them with reasons they need to do business with you.

Footprints are ways a prospect or client can find you again when/if needed. Footprints include your business card, a personal brochure, newsletter, article reprints, etc.

The objective is to make it easier for your prospects and clients to remember you and to contact you. You can accomplish this in many ways.

How will you plant triggers and leave footprints?

Enter Your Responses and Personal Action Steps

Mehdi's Success Tool # 170

You are in business. You are running your business. You are the business. So manage yourself like a business.

Evaluate your operation and include the principles of good business.

Review your use of time, your revenue flow, and where from where your profit comes. Know your categories of clients, and products. Know your **NCR** – New Client Revenue – a dollar number average for all new clients.

Should you manage certain accounts differently? Should you make adjustments?

Can you do this objectively, as a business executive?

Enter Your Responses and Personal Action Steps

Mehdi's Success Tool # 171

Do not make assumptions. Assumptions can damage your client's financial condition and endanger your personal financial health!

Do not select solutions or products in advance.

Always get sufficient financial and emotional input from your prospect before making any recommendations.

Can you refrain from answering questions until you have factored in the prospects information?

Enter Your Responses and Personal Action Steps

Mehdi's Success Tool # 172

For any sales presentation where you act as the agent, planner, or advisor, you must have complete and accurate critical information about your prospect's needs.

This is commonly known to professionals as "fact finding" but this is not such a friendly term for prospects. It seems cold and uncaring, and yet fact finding is exactly the opposite.

Do you know how to get this essential information?

Enter Your Responses and Personal Action Steps

Mehdi's Success Tool # 173

Your business today is most likely due to efforts you made several months ago. **What are you doing now that will benefit you a few months from now?**

You must plant seeds daily in your effort to grow new business in your future. This includes prospecting daily!

Make efforts that help develop your future new business even if you are doing well today.

Please explain how you will do this?

Enter Your Responses and Personal Action Steps

Mehdi's Success Tool # 174

Manage all of your sales efforts with *next steps*.

It is easier to follow a system when important tasks are broken down into smaller steps. Each step seems easier to achieve. But you must have tracking for them – sometimes referred to as your "To Do System."

Do you have an organized system, perhaps as part of your CRM program?

What does your organized system entail?

Enter Your Responses and Personal Action Steps

Mehdi's Success Tool # 175

Get information. Evaluate your information. Use or act upon the conclusions you reach. Reason! Deduct. Solve mysteries. Use your Sherlock Holmes skills to uncover your prospect's agenda or mind set. Many prospects, especially business owners or key executives in a smaller firm, have very important business-related objectives or inclinations. These will often govern all of their personal financial decisions.

For example: Discover who the decision-maker is? Get the correct name, title, address, phone number, e-mail, etc., of the decision-maker. **For what is the decision-maker responsible?**

Is useful information available to you from a website? Have you learned how to gather information on the internet?

Can you be like Sherlock Holmes regarding these and other factors?

Enter Your Responses and Personal Action Steps

Mehdi's Success Tool # 176

Have many and varied interests - and stay informed.

Be up-to-date with news events, local, regional, national and international.

Change is inevitable! **You must alter your use of these success tools to adjust for "tight money times" and perhaps "renewed inflation."**

Become a student of the world. Perhaps subscribe to a foreign publication. Being well-informed makes you more interesting and more conversational.

Do you consider yourself to be an "aware and informed" person?

Enter Your Responses and Personal Action Steps

Mehdi's Success Tool # 177

Your **positive words** have an impact that leads to opportunities for you.

Your **negative words** generally limit your opportunities.

Any lack of widespread interests can easily be interpreted by prospects to suggest that you simply do not care about other persons, and are self-centered.

This is one reason why charitable work can be valuable to your image.

How can you stay basically positive and proactive?

Enter Your Responses and Personal Action Steps

Mehdi's Success Tool # 178

Help set a goal or goals for your prospect or client. When your client reaches the goal, then you may raise the goal.

Outline the actions and time period needed to accomplish these goals.

Obtain a confirmation of these goals – in a well-organized fashion.

Can you do this in writing?

Enter Your Responses and Personal Action Steps

Mehdi's Success Tool # 179

Ask! Ask! Ask! Ask! And ask again for the appointment.

Ask for another meeting.

Ask to deliver some "additional information" or some "financial research" that might be applicable.

Ask for the order.

Can you ask?

Enter Your Responses and Personal Action Steps

Mehdi's Success Tool # 180

Do what you say! Keep your promises.

Your promise is an obligation. I repeat, your promise made is your debt unpaid. You have been told this time and again. Accept this truism as absolute.

When I hear complaints about other salespersons and financial advisors, this is the one complaint I hear most often. Too many agents and planners do not deliver as promised - or when promised. They create expectations and then fail to meet them.

Can you say what you will do… and do what you say…?

Enter Your Responses and Personal Action Steps

Mehdi's Success Tool # 181

You should transition smoothly from your small talk to your sales presentation.

Do not shock your prospect!

Do not leap into asking personal questions!

Do not be confrontational or challenging!

Can you transition smoothly?

Enter Your Responses and Personal Action Steps

Mehdi's Success Tool # 182

Here are five steps to building and maintaining trust:

- Send evidence of your status/expertise/professional success to your prospect in advance of any meeting.

- Dialogue with your prospects, by mailed handwritten notes, printed letters, e-mails, or phone calls. (Use multiple methods).

- Search in depth for specifics regarding your prospect's circumstances and needs.

- Explore possible solutions and reach agreement on what your products or services need to accomplish for your prospect.

- Explain clearly how your product or service will produce the desired solution.

Can you master these five steps?

Enter Your Responses and Personal Action Steps

Mehdi's Success Tool # 183

Learn what your prospect is willing to do to solve his or her problem.

You can ask that question, after exploring the issues and gathering information.

Often when you ask, prospects will say or admit, that they have no plans for solving the problem.

Then you are in an excellent position to ask, "Would you like me to assemble for you the types of plans that others are using to accomplish this goal? **Can you elaborate on this?**

Enter Your Elaboration and Action Steps

Mehdi's Success Tool # 184

Can you tailor everything you do with and for your prospect?

Can you make your clients believe that all of your advice and recommendations were custom developed for them?

What would be required to do this? Even small personalization, like placing their names on folders or notebooks will seem more important to them than you may realize.

Everyone likes to see their own name.

Enter Responses and Action Steps

Mehdi's Success Tool # 185

End your meeting by planning and revealing your next move.

Get your prospect or client to agree with your revealed priority and timetable.

How can you accomplish this task?

Enter Your Responses and Personal Action Steps

Mehdi's Success Tool # 186

Failure to follow-up swiftly is another leading reason that your sales may be lost.

- Slow follow-up allows clients to feel that you do not care about them

- Delayed follow-up allows clients to feel that they are not as important as other clients.

Can you follow-up until all the necessary elements are made and your sale is closed?

Enter Your Responses and Action Steps

Mehdi's Success Tool # 187

Can you think like your prospect?

This employs a technique called channeling. It uses some of the principles of Neuro-Linquistic Programming (**NLP**). **NLP** is often an excellent way to communicate more effectively with your prospects and clients. **Have you read anything about NLP?**

Can you place your mind channel parallel to that of your prospect?

Enter Your Responses and Personal Action Steps

Mehdi's Success Tool # 188

Keeping your prospect or client informed is a method of following-up.

Clients get uncomfortable when they have not heard from you.

Your clients can easily contract "Buyer's Remorse" which can become a deadly virus!

Many businesses and professionals use their Client Relationship Management (**CRM**) system to semi-automate frequent contact, both in writing, by email, by phone, and even prompting for hand written notes.

Do you have such a system in daily operation now? Did your CRM system come with all the text pre-written for you?

Can you do this? Do you need a CRM system? (see Recommended Sources)

Enter Your Responses and Personal Action Steps

Mehdi's Success Tool # 189

Always thank your prospect, displaying sincere appreciation.

- Do this even if no sale was made.
- They remain a prospect for you
- Just wait a while and re-submit your recommendation

Can you do this? Can you set up a follow-up date?

Enter Your Responses and Personal Action Steps

Mehdi's Success Tool # 190

What is unique or special about you?

- **Can you further develop some aspect of your uniqueness?**

- **Can you emphasize this aspect within your marketing?**

- Is there an effective way for you to exploit this – such as use your uniqueness to meet the types of persons you would like to do business with or be better received by your prospects?

- It is possible that you can use your uniqueness to gain more publicity, and then send that to your clients, or place evidence of desired media exposure in your media kit, or exploit your publicity in other ways.

Will you use this to position you more strongly?

Enter Your Responses and Personal Action Steps

Mehdi's Success Tool # 191

Psychologists say, "If you can execute certain positive actions every day for just 21-days then you can practice those same positive actions for years."

I repeat, if you can practice new **positive habits** each day for three weeks, then you can turn these practices into success building habits that will last for years. Developing more positive sales habits is always a goal you should have.

Can you practice new beneficial sales habits for three weeks without interruption?

Enter Your Responses and Personal Action Steps

Mehdi's Success Tool # 192

Using the Success tools included in this System has enabled me to avoid most of the stress I experienced during the outset of my long career.

We all know that stress robs you of your ability to achieve the greatness that you are capable of achieving. These simple Success tools helped me achieve top production, and as I reached higher levels, gradually I began to realize the following:

- Stress can easily assure one of failure

- Systems enable you to achieve sales greatness

- Success breeds more success

Can you avoid stress, by simply adopting these success tools, without being selective – just practicing these techniques every day?

Enter Your Responses and Personal Action Steps

Mehdi's Success Tool # 193

The primary causes of stress for financial salespersons are not unique, and when you recognize them, you have taken your first corrective step. Next you can resolve the stress factors. Your most common stress factors include:

Wasting Your Time	Lengthy Phone Conversations
Rejections	Family Pressures
Disappointments	Feeling Guilty
Fear of Failure	Personal Cash Flow Problems
Stalling by Prospects	Procrastination
Attacks by Competitors	Cancelled Appointments
Criticism by Your Peers	Difficulty Finding Good Leads
Finding Appointment Locations	Traffic Jams and Parking
Badly Written Messages	Failure to Take Good Notes

Do you understand how applying success tools will reduce many of these stressors in your life?

Enter Your Responses and Personal Action Steps

Mehdi's Success Tool # 194

Napoleon Hill advised forming a "Mastermind Group" for sharing ideas and obtaining outside stimulation.

The **MDRT** has long advocated and supported members forming a professional study group and many financial professionals attribute a portion of their success, or major production increases, to this cooperative input. Participants are often in different cities, different markets, and associated with different companies.

Can you form a trusted group of three or four highly intelligent and successful people within, or related to, your specialty? Will you take this initiative, and be a strong contributor?

Enter Your Responses and Personal Action Steps

Mehdi's Success Tool # 195

Some of the tools in this *Fast-Track* Success System are initially more relevant to you and your current situation. That does not mean the others would not be useful, merely that their implementation should be deferred. After all, you cannot do all of the items in this workbook simultaneously!

The key to your success is assured by repetition – repetition of these Success tools….

Why is this true?

How can you remind yourself daily to stay on track?

Enter Your Responses and Personal Action Steps

Mehdi's Success Tool # 196

The probability of a desired behavior being repeated by you is directly related to the positive consequences that this behavior will produce for you.

Can you explain this?

How can you place this proven fact to work for you?

Enter Your Responses and Personal Action Steps

Mehdi's Success Tool # 197

If you enjoy meeting new people, you will enjoy learning more about them, and you will especially enjoy helping them!

How can you become better at meeting new people?

Will you look forward to meeting new people every day?

Enter Your Responses and Personal Action Steps

Mehdi's Success Tool # 198

Breaking **bad habits** can be very helpful to you.

Some bad habits are well recognized as harmful, such as smoking. But others are great stressors and can damage your reputation. For example, being late for appointments, or not being carefully groomed. When you have kept a prospect or client waiting, you know that you are under immediate stress.

Can you identify your bad habits that cause you professional harm?

Can I resolve now to begin correcting them?

Enter Your Responses and Personal Action Steps

Mehdi's Success Tool # 199

Never assume that you know everything.

Never assume that you know enough.

Never assume you will not need to continue to study

Never assume you are through buying books, other tools, new software or courses.

Why?

Enter Your Responses and Planned Action Steps

Mehdi's Success Tool # 200

At this point you have completed your initial review of these *FAST-TRACK* recommendations - "initial" because you will need to review them again.

**These 200 tools will be worthless if
you do not take action to use them.**

You have moved forward in your understanding, and hopefully you will use these techniques that work well for me. **Remember, you must modify them slightly to adjust for economic changes impacting your clients.**

Continue your pursuit of knowledge and financial sales skills. The two best organizations that you can access for this are the **MDRT** and the **IARFC**. (See Recommended Sources) Both of these exclusive associations believe in **ethical, professional selling**, and they offer the collective wisdom of thousands of other successful financial advisors.

Enter Your Responses and Personal Action Steps

Implement Your Good Intentions Now – Success is Assured!

Career Profile - Mehdi Fakharzadeh

One of the most respected contributors to the financial services industry, world-wide, started his insurance career collecting premiums as a debit agent, in Hell's Kitchen – the roughest and most poverty stricken area of New York City. There were no logical reasons why a young immigrant from Iran should have succeeded in that environment, except for two things – diligent effort and great character.

Coming to America

Born on April 21, 1922, in Tehran, Iran. Mehdi's mother died when she was only 24 years old. He describes the loss of his mother as, "The biggest sorrow in my life. At the young age of seven I was devastated." He was the eldest son of Haj Ali Asghar Fakharzadeh, a real estate developer and retail store owner. Mehdi says, "My father was fantastic and I had a very close relationship with him." While his father initially discouraged his coming to America, he lived to see Mehdi become one of the most famous and most successful agents in financial products and services, extremely proud of his accomplishments in the USA.

Mehdi worked as he completed high school and then graduated from the University of Tehran College of Law. Since Iran did not offer advanced degrees at that time, he investigated Brigham Young University in Provo, Utah because their president had served Iran as an agricultural assistant.

When he arrived in New York City in 1948, he had no idea how to reach BYU. Someone pointed out the Greyhound station and after three miserable days, Mehdi arrived in Utah to enroll at BYU. He was told, "Your English isn't good enough" so he enrolled for a semester at a Wyoming high school. In 1950 he received his Master's in Economics from BYU and was offered a scholarship to the University of Washington, where he planned to get his Ph.D.

In his first week on the Seattle campus, he met a strikingly attractive food technology major from Iceland by the name of Sigrun Fridriksdottir, and immediately began his courtship. They represented an interesting contrast - Sigrun was tall, blond and beautiful and Mehdi of average height and dark skinned. She was from a cold, moist climate and he from a hot, dry one. When Sigrun transferred to Cornell in Ithaca, New York, to obtain her Master's degree in Food Technology, Mehdi followed, continuing his courtship. They got married in New York City in July 1953 after she finished at Cornell.

Mehdi continued his education at New York University. He was three courses away from earning a Ph.D. in business administration, when Sigrun announced they were expecting their first child, and that she would be leaving her position as manager for a food freezing plant. This development abruptly altered their family finances

Starting in Insurance

In 1955, at age 33, Mehdi applied for what he believed would be a temporary position with Metropolitan Life. He found the duties of collecting premiums on the book of business assigned to him in Hell's Kitchen to be very difficult and tiring. He was making some progress, but he did not enjoy the collection responsibility and he could not see a positive future.

While an academic scholar, it is fair to say that Mehdi had not met with any economic success. His first year with MetLife was not successful, but he realized how important service was to the process of selling insurance. Rather than saying, "I'm here to collect the insurance premium" he began to say, "How can I help you?" Mehdi was making friends, but earning little money.

He told Sigrun of his frustrations and she said "You should be able to enjoy your work, so try to find work more suitable for you." But Mehdi did not want to quit as a failure, and decided to prove he could succeed - and then look for other work.

After four years he was promoted from the debit route to selling policies with face values of $2,000 or more, and within a year his sales exceeded one million dollars.

Mehdi's cultural background considered it "bad form" to talk about death and at first his sales were not substantial. But "failure" was not going to be a part of his vocabulary. He couldn't quit until he was a success, and when he had achieved that success, he did not want to quit.

Achieving Success

Within five years he was promoted by MetLife to Insurance Consultant. His sales steadily grew, and in his ninth year (in 1964 at age 42) he realized he had qualified for the Million Dollar Round Table (MDRT). Since then Mehdi has never failed to attend MDRT meetings, and has spoken often. He has qualified for Top of the Table and was a charter member of the International Forum.

Every honor that could be bestowed by MetLife has been given to Mehdi – not just for sales leadership, but for his many contributions to the industry.

According to Robert Henrikson, MetLife President and Chairman, "Membership in our Hall of Fame is reserved for those individuals who have dedicated their careers to representing MetLife with pride and professionalism, and who distinguish themselves as true leaders in sales and service. The MetLife Hall of Fame is an achievement that represents the highest level of performance in providing the best quality service to clients. Only MetLife's top representatives earn this prestigious honor."

For the first time in its 140 year history, MetLife created a Lifetime Achievement Award to recognize Mehdi's unique contributions to the company, his fellow agents, his clients and to the financial services industry. Mehdi has continued his relationship with MetLife - now in his 55th year.

Mehdi has earned the most MetLife honors for "successful client development" and "successful client retention." Insurance pioneer Norman G. Levine says, "Mehdi has provided the financial products and services needed to help achieve financial freedom for many of his clients. For Mehdi's accomplishments, he has been honored with many awards across the world – awards that recognize his contributions to the financial services profession as well as to his clients."

He won the Triskelion Award for **Consistently Building Client Trust**. Mehdi has also been a President's Trophy winner, awarded to the leading representative at MetLife. In addition, Mehdi has also earned MetLife's Golden Laureate Service Award.

Mehdi has also received the highest award in financial planning – the Loren Dunton Award presented by the International Association of Registered Financial Consultants (IARFC) to those "persons who have made significant contribution to the profession of personal financial planning." Mehdi has influenced the transition within financial services as agents become advisors and elevate the complexity of their comprehensive financial services and products.

Developing His Own Style

A strong work ethic is Mehdi's guiding principle. He comments that most agents measure their work as time away from home, not time spent actually doing the essential activities. Even today, he arrives at his office at 6:30 in the morning and spends most of the day either on sales appointments or involved in some form of client contact.

Despite his intellectual and academic achievements, Mehdi believes "Good Habits equal Good Producers" and he has worked on improving his own habits for over 50 years. He devised unique and exclusive tools to enable him to accomplish this.

While Mehdi may have started on a debit route and selling small insurance policies to fill simple needs, ninety percent of his sales now involve business needs and estate planning. He contends that, **"selling a $500 debit policy is no different from a $500,000 ordinary life or substantial investment or annuity"**. In his thousands of presentations, he reminds professional audiences, "You have to meet the people on a favorable basis, gain their confidence, present the facts, and ask for the order!"

The Current Outlook

Mehdi's greatest regret is not entering insurance and financial services until age 33. "No individual producer can be an expert in every specialty area. Our business is too complex today. To achieve optimum results you need to build alliances with other agents as well as related professionals in other financial and legal areas. With accountants, bankers and attorneys, once they have an opportunity to see the quality of your work, they will in turn, introduce you to others."

Asked if he sees the opportunities for new entrants to personal financial services to be reducing, Mehdi indicated, "There are many options available today, such as financial planning, the senior market, asset gathering and the small business market. If you make the right choice (for yourself) and if you select the right selling system (for yourself) then financial services could prove to be a very lucrative career."

Does he worry about the economy? "In the midst of all this bad news there are still many businesses doing well. With unemployment at 10%, there are 90% still working. You have to change your operating and marketing a bit as other changes take place in your marketplace. You have to work a little harder, or a little longer. You have to constantly pump up your enthusiasm. But the opportunities are boundless!"

Service First and Always

Mehdi has a simple credo for his business and his lifestyle, "I love to help people in every aspect of their life. Each of my clients is a valued friend and each represents an important relationship that I treasure. They make me feel wealthy. They care about me because I care about them. Some of my clients have been with me since my first year as an agent"

Good business results follow a pattern of steady activity for Mehdi, "I was not always successful in this profession. I had a number of handicaps. I was foreign born, did not know the language and customs, did not have friends or school mates here, yet I built a successful practice."

All of his activity is client-needs based. "It is absolutely necessary for us to analyze the needs to properly identify the problem we can solve with our products. We must have a total understanding and recommend only the most appropriate solution."

He still delivers 40-50 talks per year at financial services meetings nationally and around the globe – challenging and teaching others how to achieve success by contributing value. Some are short, one hour presentations. But often the audience will not let him go. At a Worldwide Chinese Life Insurance Congress in Chengdu he was on stage for three hours. For a man of any age, much less 86 at that time, this was a testament to his energy and enthusiasm to help others.

Mehdi has been a persistent student and he applauds the IARFC continuing education requirement of 40 units yearly. "I truly emphasize and re-emphasize the value of acquiring ongoing education and knowledge the same way I did and am still doing. A professional designation, like the RFC, tells your prospects and clients that you value education and competence."

He lives by the Iranian proverb, "God blesses the one who gives advice, but God blesses a thousand times more the one who takes the advice and follows through on it."

Professional Involvement

Mehdi served as Educational Vice President for the New York Association of Life Underwriters (NYALU) and served on the Board of Directors for the MDRT Top of the Table. In addition, he has been Chairman of MetLife's President's Conference.

Mehdi's career exemplifies his commitment to ongoing learning to improve his sales and service performance and staying current with the most up-to-date information in the financial products and services industry.

During his career Mehdi has changed when his markets changed. When consumers began to prefer financial planners over insurance agents, Mehdi repositioned himself as a financial planner by earning the prestigious financial planning designation of Registered Financial Consultant (RFC) awarded by the International Association of Registered Financial Consultants (IARFC). He then went on to play a key influential role in that rapidly-growing organization of financial planners.

He has written two books, **Nothing Is Impossible** and **Everything Is Possible**, and both were industry best-sellers. He has generously shared his techniques and tools at industry conferences and in articles in professional journals outlining his concepts that good habits produce sales success.

An industry achievement for which Mehdi is especially famous is his lengthy qualification for membership in the Million Dollar Round Table and his role as a leader within the MDRT. He remains one of the MDRT's most honored and most recognized members. When he attends the meeting he is mobbed by producers who have heard him speak, and is also sought by the members of the Executive Committee, seeking his wisdom and perspective.

The MDRT is considered a premier association of insurance professionals. The members of this elite world-wide organization are insurance and financial planning professionals from around the globe who meet very high annual production requirements, adhere to strict ethical standards, and maintain their pursuit of continuing professional education.

Mehdi is both a Qualifying Member and a Life Member and he has been a frequent MDRT speaker at their annual meetings, international MDRT Experience sessions, and addresses several international MDRT conclaves every year.

A Sales Practice Pioneer

During his famous career, an enormous amount of Mehdi's time has been devoted to the study of sales tactics and creating, then later revising, new tools that lead to highly productive sales systems for various types of personalities. As such Mehdi is also one of the world's leading sales researchers on financial products and services.

More than any other sales trainer, or sales coach, Mehdi is credited with helping insurance agents and financial planners adopt effective sales systems that lead them to higher levels of sales productions. Often these included record levels of sales achievements, and his unique methods are effectively used around the world.

His audiences are constantly craving more. Because he is not a salesperson who relies on high-tech solutions and presentations, his recommendations are valuable for a new entrant into insurance or financial services – as well as to the seasoned veteran whose career needs a jump start.

In the spring of 2010, two respected journalists, Wu Chin-Chu and Wang Ting-Chi prepared a book, exclusively on Mehdi's sales techniques and service philosophy, entitled **Nothing is Impossible, Everything is Possible** distributed by Shy Mau Publishing for Chinese speaking life agents in Asia.

He is one of the four super-producers in another volume titled, **You Can Sell Like Ben, Mehdi, Norm and Ed**, which will also feature his dear friends, the late Ben Feldman, Norm Levine and Ed Morrow.

International Appeal

His hobbies include collecting antiques, cooking, and most especially, "Helping other agents and financial planners to improve their sales by enabling them to identify and use the sales success system that works best for them." Today, in many countries, books and articles are written about Mehdi and his methods.

He has spoken in over 50 countries, appearing in some countries as many as eighteen times, where he routinely receives standing ovations. The largest professional audience he ever addressed was 13,000 people. In September, 2009 he spoke in ten cities in China. In the spring of 2010 he addressed an audience of over 7,500 at the Asia Pacific Life Insurance Congress in Bangkok. Because of the high numbers of international speaking assignments he has fulfilled during his career, Mehdi ranks as "one of the world's most booked international speakers," according to the Pacific-Rim Speakers Network.

In China and other countries insurance agents have named their children after him. Mehdi who is famous for being humble, modest, and low-key says, "This is unbelievable. I feel extremely proud that people have honored me in this way. I never dreamed that books would be written about me in different languages."

The *Inspirator International* Magazine reprinted an article from the US-based *Fortune* magazine stating, "Mehdi is always willing to help others in his field. When people in financial sales ask Mehdi to help them learn to sell like he does, Mehdi cannot sleep until he helps them. He feels that he has a moral obligation to assist them by sharing what he knows and does. What he knows and does has made him a multi-millionaire."

Mehdi and Sigrun live in Teaneck, New Jersey, and they have raised three sons and a daughter. His current title is Senior Account Executive with The Wealth Financial Group, an office of MetLife, in Hackensack, New Jersey. He enjoys communicating with insurance agents and financial planners from around the world. He is ever-eager to acquire new and useful ideas and to know how you are doing using the success system that is most appropriate for you.

The Factors of Success

Mehdi's career illustrates that you do not have to start a sales career fresh out of college. It also shows that many persons destined for greatness will not leap immediately into high production. It took Mehdi nine years to achieve the minimum MDRT production.

Language, family and customs are not a barrier to success. In fact, these differences make one unique. What prospects really want to know is whether you sincerely care about them, and if you will deliver great service.

There is no mandatory retirement age for sales persons. At age 88, Mehdi still works a full schedule. When asked about his production objectives, he tells audiences, "I have no quota or production goals! I merely want to deliver good service and good products." When asked about retiring, Mehdi replies, "Thanks be to God, that I can continue to serve my fellow man. I am truly blessed!"

A young salesman asked him at a presentation in Japan, "What is the biggest policy you have sold?" Mehdi looked straight at him, smiled, and said, "I haven't sold it yet!'

Like the titles of his two earlier books, Mehdi's career proves that his success can be matched by thousands in financial services, because, after all:

Nothing is Impossible*....and....****Everything is Possible***

Countries Where Mehdi Has Addressed Professional Advisors and Agents

Argentina	Cyprus	Iran	New Zealand	Syria
Australia	Denmark	India	Norway	Taiwan
Austria	Egypt	Italy	Philippines	Thailand
Bahamas	England	Jamaica	Poland	Turkey
Bermuda	France	Japan	Puerto Rico	Taiwan
Belgium	Germany	Lebanon	Scotland	Trinidad & Tobago
Canada	Greece	Luxembourg	Singapore	United States
Czechoslovakia	Grenada	Macau	Slovakia	
China	Holland	Malaysia	South Africa	
Croatia	Hong Kong	Mexico	Spain	
Curacao	Iceland	Monaco	Sri Lanka	

Career Profile - Forrest Wallace Cato

In the book *Secrets of Wealth*, writer Parviz Firouzgar warns the American public about unscrupulous financial planners, but he chose financial planning writer/editor Cato to defend the financial planning profession. Firouzgar made this choice because Cato remains the leading advocate, promoter, and supporter of the legitimate professionals in financial planning since the inception of this specialty discipline. Cato is a very aggressive opponent of those who do not ethically serve the public. His professional motto reminds advisors they "Can Cut a Better Figure" and he often emphasizes this with swords and knives.

Public Relations Quarterly reported, "Cato is a scholar, an award-winning author, reviewer, critic, biographer, op-ed writer, lecturer, teacher, financial industry researcher, and essayist." He also works as a national and international financial magazine editor. As an award-winning journalist Cato has interviewed three Prime Ministers, the King of Thailand, the Dalai Lama, Ted Turner, Richard Branson, Sir John Templeton, Peter Lynch, Bill Gates, Warren Buffett and George Soros, among others.

Cato is credentialed as a recognized member of the media authorized to cover the Congress, Senate, and the White House. He has personally and privately interviewed five Presidents of the United States: Ronald Reagan, Jimmy Carter, Richard Nixon, Lyndon Johnson and Bill Clinton.

He has written on financial planning for the Federal Reserve Bank and for the *Funk & Wagnall's New Encyclopedia*. In his capacity as Media Advocate for financial professionals Cato has edited and enhanced hundreds of articles appearing in recognized publications under the byline of his clients.

Cato's writings have been published in the USA, Canada, Japan, South Korea, Taiwan, Hong Kong, Thailand, South Africa, Germany, Philippines, Malaysia, India, Singapore, Indonesia, China, the United Kingdom (England, Ireland, Scotland and Wales) Australia, and New Zealand.

He received the Lifetime Financial Writer's Award from the Money School of Boston, and the Financial Writer Award from the International Association for Financial Planning (IAFP, now FPA), plus the *Financial Profiles* Magazine *2005 Financial Writer of the Year Award*.

Cato is a former national headquarters member of The American Legion, is a board member of the Loren Dunton Foundation for Financial Service, and serves on the board of the National Center for Bankruptcy Accountability. Cato is a co-founder of the American-British Military Museum in Norwich, England.

He is named for General Nathan Bedford Forrest, the Confederate Cavalry hero, who won the Battle of Sacramento, which was fought near his hometown of Madisonville in Hopkins County, Kentucky. Despite the family's love of the name Forrest, his friends and clients still call him "Wally."

Entry Into Journalism

While stationed in England, he was appointed a base newspaper editor in the Strategic Air Command (SAC), under General Curtis E. LeMay. He restructured the publication to increase comprehension and readership, and that format was adopted throughout the Air Force. During this period he enrolled at Oxford University, which was located near the SAC base where Cato was assigned.

In Germany he interviewed many infamous Nazi leaders, including Albert Speer, and he studied the deception and propaganda techniques used by the National Socialists and Hitler to shape the opinions of the German people. This was chronicled in his first book, *Nazi,* which sold out all copies. He became a personal friend of Simon Wiesenthal, the famous Nazi hunter for whom the Holocaust Museum was named.

After the Air Force, he was hired by Colonel Tom Parker, to help promote a totally unknown singer, Elvis Presley. During his Nashville days Cato's best friend was Ray Walker, a member of the Jordanaires singing group, which backed-up Elvis. He also wrote album cover copy for many singers.

Cato edited many scripts for movies and early television shows, becoming very familiar with "stars" such as Sandra Dee and the legendary cowboy star, Roy Rogers. He learned how to get in to see politicians, publishers, producers, editors and how to present his clients' proposition. This talent, how to get past the gatekeepers, enables him to swiftly achieve attention for clients, in entertainment or financial services.

Media Advocacy Services

Cato has served for 28-years as a media advocate for financial planners, VIP-financial types, senior executives, insurance agents, and famous professionals in eleven countries. For these "names" Cato obtains local, regional, national, and international targeted media exposures (valuable publicity).

For clients he creates, establishes, and maintains, desired images within target markets. This proven sales and marketing communications effort leads to the increased understanding that results in greater acceptance for the financial products or services provider.

He arranges for financial planners to serve on the boards of corporations, foundations, associations, educational institutions, and public committees.

Editorial Positions

Cato is former Editor-in-Chief of *Financial Planning* magazine, the flagship publication of the IAFP, *Trusts & Estates: Journal of Wealth Management, Financial Services Advisor,* the *Fraternal Monitor*, and the *Inspirator International*, the largest circulation English language magazine in the Pacific-Rim countries, devoted to sales training, personal improvement, and money management. He has also been Associate Editor of *Pension World* Magazine, and former Contributing Editor to *Oil & Gas Tax Quarterly* Magazine. He is currently the International Editor for *Advisers* magazine, published in China

Consumer Publications

He has written for such consumer publications as *Reader's Digest, The New York Times, Money, U.S. News & World Report, Newsweek, Income Opportunities, New York, Popular Science, Better Homes & Gardens, Popular Mechanics, Parade, World Executive Digest, Modern Maturity,* and others.

Financial Publications

His financial writings have appeared in major financial trade and professional publications such as *The Wall Street Journal, Financial Times, Tax Shelter Digest, Barron's, Asian Investor, Medical Economics, Global Finance, The Journal of Finance, Investment Dealers' Digest, Agri-Finance, Investor's Business Daily, Finance Asia, Wealth And Retirement Planner, Broker Dealer, Annuity Selling Guide and Popular Financing.*

Banking Publications

Cato has been published in such banking publications as *American Banker, Banking Today, United States Banker, Mid-Western Banker, Oklahoma Banker, Bank Marketing, Texas Bankers Record, Mississippi Banker, Mississippi Banker, Hoosier Banker,* and *Mid-Continent Banker.*

Real Estate Publications

Magazines publishing Cato's real estate articles include *National Real Estate Investor, The Hawaiian Realtor, New England Real Estate Journal, Orange County Apartment News, Real Estate Business, Real Estate Forum, Real Estate News, Real Estate Review, Real Estate Today, Realtor News, Southeast Real Estate Today, Realtor News, Southeast Real Estate News, Tennessee Realtor, Realty,* plus many articles appearing in newspaper supplements.

Oil and Gas Publications

His writings have been featured in such oil and gas magazines as *Oil & Gas Investor, Oil & Gas Tax Quarterly, Gulf Coast Oil World, Northeast Oil World, Drill Bit, Western Oil World,* and additional publications.

Insurance Publications

Cato has written for such insurance journals as *Life Insurance Selling, Broker World, Mid-America Insurance, New England Insurance Times, Insurance Marketing, New England Insurance Times, California Insurance, National Underwriter, Round the Table, Agents Sales Journal* and other publications serving the insurance profession.

Financial Planning

His writings have been published in *Financial Planning, Financial Services Advisor, Trusts & Estates, Financial Profiles, Pension World, Fraternal Monitor, Probe, Annuity Super Producer, Leaders, Institutional Investor, Journal of Finance, Financial & Estate Planners Quarterly, Investment Dealer's Digest, Registered Representative, Financial Advisor* and *Horses Mouth.*

His monthly column, *Cato Comments About Your Image,* is a popular feature in *The IARFC Register,* and it receives frequent reader responses.

Specialty Publications

Cato's other published credits include such specialty titles as *The American Salesman, Popular Mechanics, Variety, Business Screen, Shooting Times, Hollywood Reporter, Public Relations Quarterly, Florida Today, Parade, Kentucky,* and more.

Public Relations Writing

- The National Investor Relations Institute (NIRI)
- The Investment Company Institute (ICI)
- Financial Public Relations Association (FPRA)
- International Association of Registered Financial Consultants (IARFC)
- The American Bankers Association (ABA)

Image Building Activities for Clients

Obtaining and placing stars on the Hollywood Walk of Fame.
Placing client's names in lights on Broadway.
Ghostwriting and promoting books for famous celebrities.
Scripting original motion picture stories and screenplays.
Creating direct mail packages.
Writing subscription direct mail pieces for Playboy and Readers Digest

Preparing circulation solicitations for Nightingale-Conant
Speech writing for VIP-types.
Writing scripts for audiocassettes, CDs, PowerPoints, and videos.
Writing scripts for TV infomercials.
Arranging White House visits with the United States' President.
Arranging appointments to Presidential commissions.
Arranging appointments Governors' Committees.
Arranging for executives to serve on boards of directors.
Arranging for "rides" aboard Air Force One.
Arranging for celebrities to serve as chairmen or spokespersons for charities, non-profits, or foundations.
Arranging personality guest appearances on radio and television.

Presentations and Lectures

- New York Publicity Club
- The Florida Savings and Loan League
- The Armed Forces Information Officer's Association
- Chicago Public Relations Society
- The American Bankers Association (ABA)
- The American Management Association
- The Public Relations Society of America (PRSA)
- Hollywood Publicity Club
- Various IAFP (now FPA) Conventions
- The IARFC Annual Forum
- The London Chamber of Commerce
- The Thailand Stock Exchange
- The Pacific-Rim Speakers Network (P-RSN)

This often-quoted financial planning media advocate has spoken to additional associations or organizations serving financial professionals, public relations practitioners, celebrity promoters, artist's managers, direct mail copywriters, fund raisers, USA military organizations, foundation directors, and other financial related groups.

He is a senior fellow in Financial Planning Media Advocacy at the Al-Habtoor School of Business in Dubai. He also teaches public relations, image management and marketing to the media at the Insurance Pro Shop and has spoken at the Altmann Financial Sales Mastermind Group in Madison, WI.

Five books ghost-written by Cato (for clients) made *The New York Times* top-ten best seller list. The published articles drafted by advisors and agents, that have been edited, polished and placed by Cato, number in the hundreds.

Many financial advisors have brought their rough manuscripts to Cato, with the plea to have it edited, packaged and presented to publishers. Of course this is a confidential relationship and his name does not appear on those works – which probably never would have been published, had it not been for his efforts.

During the annual IARFC Financial Advisors Forum he presents The Cato Award for "accomplishments with published writing that promotes greater understanding for and appreciation of financial planning."

Cato and Ed Morrow jointly present the Image-Branding Workshop an exclusive program for financial service professionals, based on techniques and practices created over twenty-eight years of successful experience as a media advocate/journalist and practice management/marketing coach and literary agent.

Cato Introductions to Classic Books

How To Sell Your Way Through Life by **Napoleon Hill**, author of the motivational classic *Think & Grow Rich*.

Financial Planning As I Created It by **Loren Dunton**, co-founder of the multi-trillion dollar financial planning industry.

My First 65-Years In Advertising by **Maxwell B. Sackheim**, Direct Mail Hall-of-Fame.

Self-Improvement Through Public Speaking by **Orison Swett Marden**, author of the all-time best-selling book on effective public speaking.

Make Your Walls Tumble by **BBC-TV** personality Rev. Dr. John Lutwyche Clemens.

Financial Planning As I Conceived It by financial planning pioneer John B. Keeble, III

How To Sell And Service Nine Out Of Ten by Lew Nason, LUTCF, FMM, RFC

Helping Clients Can Make You Rich by insurance agent Sid Friedman

The Science of Getting Rich by Wallace D. Wattles.

Tremendous People I Have Loved by Charles "Tremendous" Jones RFC,

How To Advertise Yourself by Maxwell B. Sackheim, founder of the **Book-Of-The-Month Club** and the world's all-time most successful direct mail copywriter

Your Book of Financial Planning by the co-founder of the financial planning profession, Loren Dunton.

Books by Cato

You Can Sell Like Ben, Mehdi, Norm & Ed, What It Takes To Make You Great, Napoleon Hill Heroes, Sales Promotional Image Building, and Beware of Financial Planning Clowns! distributed by the IPS Publishing Group, containing over fifty-five interviews with leading financial planners. This is the first publication that examines `clowns' in the financial planning profession.

Cato's other books include *The Plain Language Law Library*, containing six volumes, one each on *Corporations, Civil Procedures, Civil Wrongs, Crimes, Criminal Procedure, Agency And Partnerships*, all volumes co-written with a team of seven attorneys.

His book *The Five International Success Laws* is included in the book *Four Great Timeless Success Classics*, along with *As a Man Thinketh, A Message to Garcia*, and *Secrets From the Richest Man In Babylon*.

Loren Dunton, co-creator of the multitrillion dollar financial planning movement, in his book **Financial Planning: A New Profession**, wrote, "Cato has a national reputation as an editor, journalist, and media promotion genius. He's written more copy to help gain acceptance, understanding, and appreciation for financial planners than any other person in America!"

Cato is featured in the books **A Passion for Compassion: the Proven Formula for Successful Financial Advisors** by insurance legend Norman G. Levine, RFC and he is profiled in **The Sales Slump Doctor Is In** by psychologist Mickey M. Greenfield, JD, Ph.D.

Cato creates, establishes, and maintains desired images to help achieve marketing objectives for financial professionals in nine countries. When not negotiating with editors and publishers, he can be reached at:

Intergroup II/Atlanta, Inc.
915 River Rock Drive, Suite 101
Woodstock, GA 30188-9334
USA

Phone: **770 516 9395**
E-mail: **ForrestCato01@BellSouth.net**
Website: **CatoMakesYouFamous.com**

Career Profile - Edwin P. Morrow

Ed Morrow received his education (in English Literature) at Centre College in Danville, Kentucky and at the University of Louisville School of Law. His education was interrupted by military service, where he started as a private and ended up as an airborne qualified infantry officer. After separation from the service, he began his business career as a financial analyst for Dun & Bradstreet. However, he soon became frustrated writing about successful business owners, and wanted a more challenging and remunerative position for himself.

In 1964 the economy in Louisville was not doing well, and his friends expressed amazement when he indicated he had tendered his resignation. But he was not deterred, telling them he had placed a *Situation Wanted* ad in the *Courier Journal* and he soon expected to receive job offers. This met with derision....until his ad received 85 replies in 4 days!

Selecting a New Career

He was offered a position with US Gypsum, including a car and generous expense allowance, but there was a strict territorial limit and the company had a practice of periodically reducing the territory of those who met with success, a practice also popular with pharmaceutical firms. Their regional manager said, "Why not consider life insurance? That is what my brother does in Michigan, and he makes REAL money!" So Ed retrieved all of the ad responses from insurance firms "filed" in his waste basket and he started calling. Despite knowing only a few people in Louisville, and despite being a single man who owned no insurance, investments, or real estate, he was offered several positions. He ultimately ended up selecting Equitable Life since a former Army buddy, Mel Gregory, was there, and the young agency manager, Jack Kinder, had an aggressive training program

In less than three years Ed was appointed unit manager, supervising marketing and training in estate planning and employee benefits. He became a Chartered Life Underwriter within three years and moved to Middletown, Ohio, a town of 45,000. He began charging fees in 1967, a practice that amazed (and displeased) his associates at Equitable. In 1969 he founded Financial Planning Consultants, Inc to offer fee-based services, specializing in planning for corporate executives and business owners. The firm is now engaged in software, training, education and consulting for the financial services profession.

Because a new manager in Dayton did not appreciate his fee-based activity, and made fun of his early involvement with computers, Ed left that company and joined the legendary Bill Earls of Cincinnati. Ed explains, "Earls had been one of the youngest presidents of MDRT, and he had very firm standards. All agents must become MDRT, and they could select any market, as long as their persistency was close to perfect. Bill told me, I don't care about your fees, or those computer things, just do good clean business in an honorable way!" He encouraged Ed to be more active in teaching LUTC courses and to rise through the ranks to become president of the 5,000 member Ohio Association of Life Underwriters.

Professional Education and Contributions

Ed is a Chartered Life Underwriter, Chartered Financial Consultant, Certified Financial Planner, Certified Estate Planner, and Registered Financial Consultant. In 1997 he was recognized as a CT - by the International Board of Certified Trainers. He has served as an adjunct instructor in financial planning at Purdue University, Miami University of Ohio and Wright State University.

He appears regularly on Estate Planning Councils and at business seminars, including the Financial Planning Association, National Association of Insurance and Financial Advisors, CLU Institutes, the Worldwide Chinese Life Insurance Congress, International Dragon Awards, and is a frequent speaker for the Million Dollar Round Table.

Personal Financial Planning Pioneer

His first markets for comprehensive financial planning were to Southwestern Ohio small business owners, farmers, steelworkers and professionals. His fee-based plans ranged in complexity and fees from $750 to $1,500 in the early 1970s. But as Morrow's use of computer tools enabled him to improve the quality of the plans, the fee levels increased, and the scope of the analysis improved. He began to offer financial planning to the key executives of small companies, with follow-up implementation with insurance products.

In 1976 the firm offered a Group IRA plan to the U.S. employees of an international association, and this led to providing individual planning services to many of those covered under these new retirement accounts permitted under ERISA.

A Record Accomplishment

In 1980 Ed presented comprehensive planning as an executive perquisite for the leadership of Armco Steel, the largest employer in the immediate area. This became what was most thought at the time, to be the the largest fee-based engagement - encompassing 136 senior executives at a fee of about $6,000 each, plus the mid-range managers for fees ranging from $2,400 to $3,600. His firm employed the active participation of local CPA tax specialists, estate planning attorneys and a trust company investment officer.

Gradually this service was expanded to more public companies, such as Mead Paper, Procter & Gamble, Delta Airlines (Comair), Smucker's, the Cincinnati Medical Association, the Ohio Hospital Association and the Cincinnati-based Escort Radar

Detector manufacturer. Often Ed used the interlinking nature of corporate directorships to go from one company to another.

As the Pension Reform Act caused the termination of many qualified plans, the firm launched into offering group annuities as a funding source, handling in excess of $100 million transferred into IRAs and annuity certificates.

These activities also spawned a study group on financial planning that coalesced under Ed's leadership into Confidential Planning Services, an amalgamation of firms that all wanted to offer fee-based financial planning to professionals and corporate executives. According to Ed, "Confidential Planning should have acquired or been acquired by a securities broker dealer, because we lacked the control and revenue collection possibilities that would have been offered. Gradually the various companies went their own way, into profitable, but local, individual services."

Morrow's financial career continued to thrive and he eventually became the foremost financial planning ambassador to the world, actually introducing and establishing personal financial planning in China, Asia, parts of Europe, and most Pacific-Rim countries, now under the auspices of the IARFC where he is Chairman and CEO.

Professional Writing

Twenty-two training manuals for financial planning, practice management and marketing have been authored by Ed, focusing on the career opportunities in personal financial planning. For eight years he hosted a weekly radio show "Money Talks" originating from WPFB in Middletown and he prepared weekly columns for Ohio newspapers. Today, he is a monthly contributor for *Popular Financing* magazine published in Beijing, China.

He serves on the editorial boards of the *Journal of Financial Service Professionals*, the *Journal of Personal Finance*, *Probe* newsletter, the *Register* magazine, *Popular Financing*, and is one of the "Expert Contributors" for *ProducersWEB.com*.

He contributed to the MDRT *Annuity Sales Manual*, the MDRT *Information Retrieval Index*, NAIFA's Agent Website and wrote the *Practice Management Guide* for the ICFP.

A prolific author of over 1,000 articles on practice management and financial planning in professional journals, five books on practice management, and eight software programs used by over 5,000 financial planners, accountants and educators.

ProPlan (now Plan Builder) comprehensive financial planning software was released in 1980 is in use by about 600 planning firms. Practice Builder, which includes a Master Implementation Checklist of 750 planning techniques and over 5,000 pages of financial information, is a widely used CRM program for financial advisors. Another software program, Client Builder, a presentation system, enables advisors to secure new fee-based planning engagements.

He authored **Computerizing Your Financial Planning Practice** published by the College for Financial Planning. In 1998 he co-authored, with Jeffrey Kelvin, **The**

Complete Millennium Preparation Guide for Financial Advisors. In 1999 he produced ***Personal Coaching for Financial Advisors***, a reference guide for planners and in 2009 the IARFC published six texts, to which he contributed material, as part of their intensive Financial Planning Process course. His articles, books and presentations have made him internationally regarded as "an advisor to financial advisors" for which he received the Cato Award for excellence in financial journalism.

Software and Technology Leader

At the outset of his career Ed recognized how technology could advance the delivery of financial services, beginning with a thirty-four pound Divisuma mechanical calculator costing $868 used to assemble multi-policy illustrations. This was soon replaced with one of the first four-function Casio hand models. In 1967 he acquired a tape-drive Olivetti word processor, and then a dual cassette Wang, for documents and mass mailings. For calculations he acquired a "dumb terminal" using the Control Data time-sharing system.

In 1970 he purchased a KeyPact terminal from Computone Systems, and began writing application programs for them. In 1972 he acquired the first of several DEC WD78 units, that enabled him to have five programs written for insurance advisors. In 1977 he purchased a multi-terminal CPM operating system Micromation computer that contained large processor boards and GW Basic, the fore-runner of Microsoft Basic installed in 1978.

When the IBM PC was introduced he purchased the first XT unit in Ohio which included a small hard drive, and began the software translation from Micromation and Apple, to the PC. The Novell network in the FPC building was stretching beyond the 16 terminal capacity as the firm continued the programming of the applications Ed designed for delivering financial plans to small businesses and corporate executives. Of the seven application programs, three revised and updated versions are still in service. Ed is presently revising the Client Builder presentation software and internet delivery applications

Professional Service

Ed has headed the Continuing Education Committee for the Society of Financial Service Professionals and served as the founding President of the Miami Valley Society of the ICFP. He served as a national director of the Academy of Financial Services, the Institute of CFP, and for three years he chaired the Financial Advisors Section of the National Association of Insurance & Financial Advisors (NAIFA).

He currently serves as Chairman and Chief Executive Officer of the International Association of Registered Financial Consultants, a non-profit association, which under his leadership has increased membership from 648 to over 8,000 and includes members in 31 nations.

Ed commenced delivery of fee-based financial plans in 1967, and was a very close associate of Loren Dunton, in the development of the financial planning profession. In his writings Dunton called Ed, "The co-founder of financial planning." Loren focused on developing the domestic institutions, using much of Ed's materials, while Ed concentrated on professional articles, software, and the international expansion of the profession. Dunton passed away in 1997, just before a tribute Ed planned for him at Stanford University. Ed was later presented with the Loren Dunton Memorial Award for his contributions to the financial planning profession.

He has been selected by *Money Magazine* as one of "the leading financial planners in the U.S." In 1992 Ed was appointed "Practitioner in Residence" at Wright State University, for three years, to enhance its financial services curriculum, under a grant from the Cleveland Foundation

Presentations and Instruction

Ed is a frequent presenter at national conferences of professional associations, insurance companies and broker/dealers - on topics such as: "Practice Management" "Strategic Marketing Solutions," "Adding Fee-Based Income," "Personal Coaching," "Technology Applications," "Trust Financial Advisors and Trust Protectors," "Web-Based Marketing," "Client Relationship Marketing," and the "Fast-Start Workshop."

Due to his involvement, presentations and course lecturing on financial planning in 21 countries, including Australia, Malaysia, Thailand, China, Taiwan, Trinidad, Greece, Canada and Bermuda, Ed was recognized by *Who's Who in Business Worldwide*. Still a resident of Middletown, Ed is the founder and past president of the Sorg Opera Company, and is quite proud of his three children: Kate, who he claims is the quintessential mother, Susan, a software executive with a digital printing pioneer firm, and Ed III who is the Wealth Management Communications Specialist for Key Bank, holding a JD, LLM, MBA, RFC, CFP and is currently a Ph.D. candidate.

Ed welcomes your thoughts and suggestions about this course or your career.

    Edwin P. Morrow, ChFC, CFP, CLU, CEP, CT, RFC
    Chairman and CEO
    International Association of Registered Financial Consultants
    Financial Planning Building
    2507 North Verity Parkway
    Middletown, Ohio 45042-0506

    Phone: **800 532 9060**
    E-Mail: **edm@IARFC.org**
    Website: **www.IARFC.org**

About Your Image

This book is about how you can improve your personal **Fast-Track** toward success. It does not include any technical coverage of personal finance, insurance or investments. But as you were reading the career profiles of Mehdi and Ed, I am sure you were fascinated by their achievements – just as I was. I have edited a number of publications in financial services, so I have encountered thousands of your peers.

There is a common denominator – most have had little or no success in enhancing their image within their market area. This is because they have not taken the simple and inexpensive steps to do this. I asked both Mehdi and Ed this question, "What could you have done, early in your career that would have advanced you even further and faster?"

I made no efforts to manage my image. When my first books were published, I did not take advantage of their publicity value. Nor did I ever use the articles that referenced me. I did all my prospecting the hard way. Had I paid more attention to my image, and to my brand, I could have sold even more insurance, to a wider market. I should have made greater efforts to develop my image and expand it to the business community.

Mehdi Fakharzadeh, MS, CLTC, RFC

The only image building effort I made in early years was involvement in professional associations – NAIFA, SFSP, ICFP, FPA, MDRT but these people were not prospects for me. The Dayton Daily News *did a Sunday Supplement cover article on me, and I was so stupid that I bought only 5 copies! I could have used this to enter wider and more profitable markets, but I failed to recognize the value, and this cost me lots of sales.*

Ed Morrow, CLU, ChFC, CT, CEP, CFP, RFC

Prepare your own Career Profile – just like those of Mehdi and Ed – and be sure it conveys your unique background and all of your achievements. Your profile is just one image-building step. Your clients will be proud to have chosen you as their advisor, and it will work wonders to increase referrals.

Recommended Sources

Professional Associations

Million Dollar Round Table (MDRT) John Prast, CEO 325 West Touhy Avenue Park Ridge, IL 60068-4265 847 692 6378 www.MDRT.org prast@MDRT.org	**International Association of Registered Financial Consultants (IARFC)** Edwin P. Morrow, Chairman and CEO Financial Planning Building 2507 North Verity Parkway Middletown, OH 45042-0530 800 532 9060 www.IARFC.org edm@IARFC.org
National Association of Insurance and Financial Advisors (NAIFA) Susan Waters, CEO 2901 Telestar Court Falls Church, VA 22042 703 770 8100 www.NAIFA.org swaters@naifa.org	**General Agents and Managers Association (GAMA)** Jeffrey Hughes, CEO 2901 Telestar Court, Suite 140 Falls Church, VA 22042 800 345 2687 www.GAMAweb.com jhughes@gamaweb.com
Society of Financial Services Professionals (SFSP) Joe Frack, CEO 19 Campus Boulevard, Suite 100 Newtown Square, PA 19073-3230 610 526 2500 www.FinancialPro.org jfrack@financialpro.org	**Association for Advanced Life Underwriting (AALU)** David Stertzer, CEO 2901 Telestar Court Falls Church, VA 22042 703 641 9885 www.AALU.org stertzer@aalu.org
Financial Planning Association (FPA) Marv Tuttle, CEO 4100 E. Mississippi Avenue Denver, CO 80246-3053 404 845 0011 www.FPAnet.org marv.tuttle@fpanet.org	**Life Insurance Foundation for Education (LIFE)** Marv Feldman, CEO 1655 N. Fort Meyer Drive, Suite 610 Arlington, VA 22209 888 543 3777 www.LifeHappens.org mfeldman@lifehappens.org

Training & Education

Kinder Brothers International (KBI)
(management training & education)
William B. Moore
17110 Dallas Parkway, Suite 220
Dallas, TX 75248
800 372 7100
www.KBIGroup.com
wmoore@KBIgroup.com

Learning Institute for Financial Executives   (LIFE)
William J Nelson, President
3195 Dayton-Xenia Road, Suite 900-385
Beavercreek, OH 45434-6200
937 506 4088
www.NelsonLearningInstitute.com
BillN@nelsonlearninginstitute.com

Financial Planning Consultants (FPC)
(Plan writing and CRM training)
Mark J. Terrett,
Financial Planning Building
2507 North Verity Parkway
Middletown, OH 45042-0430
800 666 1656
www.FinancialSoftware.com
Mark@FinancialSoftware.com

The Virtual Assistant/ Financial Services Online
(Internet-based training & support tools)
William O'Quin, President
2651 Kleinert Avenue
Baton Rouge, LA 70806-6823
(225) 387-9845
http://vsa.fsonline.com
boquin@ix.netcom.com

College for Financial Planning
The Apollo Group
8000 E. Maplewood Ave, Suite 200
Greenwood Village, CO 80111-4707
800 237 9990
www.CFFP.edu
www.cffpinfo.com

Planipedia
(Source for Financial Services Info.)
c/o PlanPlus, Inc.
Shawn Brayman, President
55 W. Mary Street, Suite 200
Lindsay, ON K9V 5Z6, Canada
800 364 1293
www.planipedia.org

The American College
Larry Barton, President
270 Bryn Mawr Avenue
Bryn Mawr, PA 19010
610 526 1000
www.theamericancollege.edu
contact@theamericancollege.edu

Life Insurance Management & Research Association (LIMRA)
Robert A. Kerzner, President & CEO
300 Day Hill Road
Windsor, CN 06095
860 688 3358
www.LIMRA.com
infocenter@LIMRA.com

Sales Support

Practice Builder Financial (CRM) **Plan Builder** (comprehensive plans) Financial Planning Consultants P. O. Box 430 Middletown, OH 45043-0430 800 111 1656 www.FinancialSoftware.com sales@financialsoftware.com	**The Covenant Group** 　(personal coaching) Norm Trainor, CEO 372 Bay Street, Suite 1201 Toronto, ONT M5H 2W9 416 204 0332 www.covenantgroup.com norm@covenantgroup.com
Response Mail Express 　(mailings and appointments) Jorge Villar, President 4910 Savarese Circle Tampa, FL 33634 800 795 2273 www.responsemail.com Bgrolemund@responsemail.com	**Insurance Pro Shop** 　(training programs and sales tools) Lewis Nason, RFC, President 150 Watson Drive Dallas, GA 30132-3700 770 443-2852 www.insuranceproshop.com lnason@insuranceproshop.com
Red Zone Marketing 　(Marketing & Practice Management) Maribeth Kuzmeski, President 1509 N. Milwaukee Avenue Libertyville, IL 60048 847 367 4066 www.redzonemarketing.com mk@redzonemarketing.com	**Senior Care Associates, inc.** 　(Long Term Care & Critical Illness) Wilma Anderson, President P.O. Box 631940 Littleton, CO 80164 720 344 0314 www.criticalilnesscoach.com Wilma@criticalillness.com

Image Building

Intergroup II/Atlanta, Inc. Forrest Wallace Cato, CEO 915 River Rock Drive, Suite 101 Woodstock, GA 30188-5338 770 516 9395 www.CatoMakesYouFamous.com forrestcato01@BellSouth.net	**The Brand Artist** Mark Patterson 525 Athens Place Westfield, IN 46074 317 536 5440 www.TheBrandArtist.com mpatterson@thebrandartist.com

Fast-Track Success Workshop

The material presented in Mehdi's Fast-Track Success System is unique in many ways: **Easily read.** Works for producers in **all markets**. Works for producers at **all experience levels**. Works for **agents and planners of all ages**. Procedures are **non-technical**. Not related to specific **products**.

This outstanding system represents the culmination of experience, ideas and techniques forming the tools that have caused Mehdi to become one of the world's most successful life insurance agents and financial advisors.

The weakness to any book is that even well-intentioned purchasers may not read it. They will start, but become distracted. They will encounter ideas that seem too technical or not applicable to their particular practice style, market or typical products.

Unfortunately, this causes them to set the book aside, and not continue – which would keep them from learning the next concept – which might be exactly what they might need. The solution is **involvement** and **initiation**. When presented in a workshop, there is great opportunity for dialogue with the presenter and with other participants. Furthermore, all of the attendees will get started on preparing their Personal Action Checklists.

Goals of the *Fast-Track* Success Workshop

- Help each participant identify their personal priorities
- Determine the tools that should be implemented first
- Become aware of recommended sources
- Learn how to prepare a personal Action Checklist
- Get started preparing their initial Action Checklist

Workshop Presentation Format

You may present a *Fast-Track* Success Workshop – as part of a special event such as an educational conference or annual meeting for leading producers. Or you might prefer a special workshop, just on this material.

Time Allocation. This is entirely up to you, but we recommend a half day session, which might be 8:30 – 12:00 or perhaps 1:00 to 4:30. Usually the first half hour is used for registration, distribution of workbooks and other materials, and introductions. *Special note: If the session is translated on an alternate speaker/translator basis, more time should be allowed.*

Room Set-up. Because the participants will be using the large book, and writing notes and preparing their personal action checklists, then a classroom style set-up is preferred, with attendees seated behind tables.

Here is how *Fast-Track* workshop has worked most effectively:

- Each participating attendee will receive a copy of Mehdi's Fast-Track Success System.

- The highlights of the book are reviewed during the session.

- A selection of Success Tools will be covered in detail. The number will depend on the time you allocate, and the audience questions.

- The use of the checklists will be covered in detail, and each person will be asked to start making entries for their immediate use.

- Participants will (optionally) receive a plastic stand in which to place their personal Action Checklist to serve as a constant reminder.

These workshops can be conducted in several locations, depending on the number of those you wish to impact.

We will also include some follow-up messages you can send by mail or email – to reinforce the messages of changing habits.

Mehdi's *Fast-Track* Workshop Suitability

• Life Insurance Companies	• Non-Profit Professional Associations
• Securities Broker Dealers	• Banking, Savings and Credit Unions
• Trust or Wealth Management Firms	• Producer Study/Mentorship Groups

Experience Counts!

Experience Counts! An event presentation source is needed by firms in the financial services industry. We can arrange for outstanding live multi-media sessions that are proven to magnify the success of individual producers or advisors. **Experience Counts!** offers these services for:

- Life Insurance Companies
- Securities Broker Dealers
- Trust or Wealth Management Firms
- Non-Profit Professional Associations
- Banking, Savings and Credit Unions
- Producer Study/Mentorship Groups

Please review these suggestions – and let us know about your group and your goals.

Authorship Counts!

Great speakers, meaning those with a strong history of personal success and independent thinking, are often the authors of books, manuals or articles that embody their principles and examples. What does your audience want? Books often go unread. The purchaser has good intentions, to read and employ the entire text. But when to start? Often one must read the entire book sequentially to reach the conclusions and determine whether the concepts are marketable. But great thought has been given to include in-depth treatment of all the major issues.

Understanding Counts!

Reading a well-written book is valuable, but the more complex the material, the slower the reading goes. Many books are unread beyond the Introduction, preface and first chapters. Many persons who are vitally interested in the topic do not learn best by reading. They prefer *seeing* the highlights and *hearing* the recommendations and *feeling* their personal responses.

Presentation Counts!

Great producers are outstanding presenters, but often they face a conflict – how to provide the audience with understanding, all the detailed evidence, and still be entertaining? PowerPoint bullet points and graphs serve to clarify concepts, but are useless for detail. Nothing is worse that a reproduction of the visual slides, that have already been viewed by the audience.

Your Three-Way Solution!

Your organization will receive a comprehensive solution. You can purchase and distribute at your event, the full text – printed in an inexpensive, easily read, paper-back format. The materials are bound at 8.5" x 11". Desired pages can be photocopied and used immediately. Select materials, designed for quick adoption, can be placed on a CD or on your website in immediately usable form, without having to be re-keyed, just edited as needed.

Language Counts!

With sufficient time, the texts and presenter PowerPoint visuals can be translated and the stage presentation delivered in either simultaneous mode or using a translator on a tag-team basis.

Tell Us What You Would Like!

Please complete the form below. There is no obligation, but we will evaluate your needs and suggest recommendations and options. **Experience Counts!** delivers memorable events....

Contact: _____ Title: _____

Firm Name: _____

Address: _____

_____

Phone: _____ Fax: _____

Email: _____ Website: _____

Presentation Logistics

Location of the Event(s): _____

Considering repeats, in several offices, different cities or countries? ☐ Yes ☐ No

Anticipated Date(s): _____

Audience size: _____ Is this a Multi-City Tour? _____

Attendees: ☐ producers only ☐ local managers ☐ regional managers
            ☐ national managers ☐ company officers ☐ other professionals

Is this for certain class producers or production club members? ☐ Yes ☐ No

Material to be presented: ☐ In English ☐ Other _____

Subject Desired: _____

Special Concern/Goal: _____

Presenter: ☐ **Mehdi Fakharzadeh** ☐ **Norm Levine** ☐ **Ed Morrow**

☐ **Forrest Wallace Cato** ☐ Other _____

Experience Counts! Marion Starr, Executive Director   Starr309@Charter.net
1189 Weaver Branch Road   Phone: **1 423 741 8224**
Bluff City, TN 37618-2547   Fax: **1 888 265 8727**

You have reached the end.

But, There is No End to Your Opportunity for Improvement!

Please don't put this workbook away. keep it handy and continuously refer to the habits and practices that you have vowed to improve. You will be amazed at the self-improvement.

Information Opportunities

We have received responses from the initial *Fast-Track* readers, "What is Next?" and "Please tell me more…" and "How are others using this…?"

Therefore, we would like to offer you the opportunity to register for periodic updates to Mehdi's *Fast-Track* Success System. **There is no charge…!**

Please complete this form. You can remove it from the book and mail it. You can fax a copy. Or you can just email the basic information to us:

    Fax to: **513 424 5752**

    Mail to: **Intergroup II / Atlanta, Inc**.
                 915 River Rock Drive, Suite 101
                 Woodstock, GA 30188-5338

    Email to: **Info@MehdiFast-Track.com**

Name: _____

Designations: _____

E-Mail: _____

Firm: _____

Street: _____

City: _____ ST: ____ Code: _____

What primary products or services do you now offer to your clients?

    ☐ Life Insurance   ☐ Annuities   ☐ Health Insurance

    ☐ Long Term Care   ☐ Critical Illness   ☐ Group Benefit Plans

    ☐ Portfolio Management   ☐ Mutual Funds   ☐ Individual Securities

    ☐ Fee-Based Plans   ☐ Business Planning   ☐ Estate Planning

    ☐ _____   ☐ _____   ☐ _____